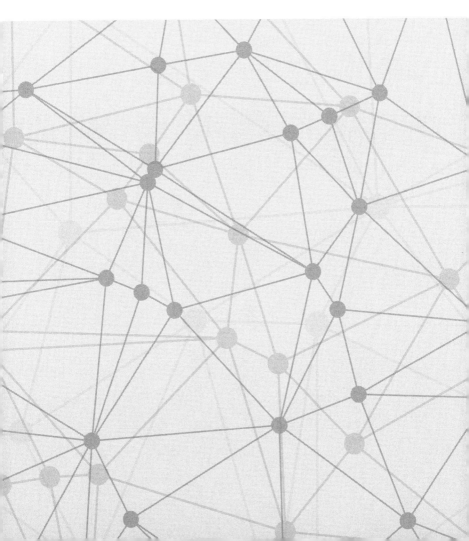

THE NEVER-ENDING
DIGITAL JOURNEY

THE NEVER-ENDING DIGITAL JOURNEY

Creating new consumer experiences through technology

Andrés Angelani
Guibert Englebienne
Martín Migoya

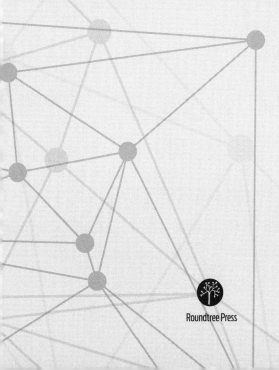

Roundtree Press

CONTENTS

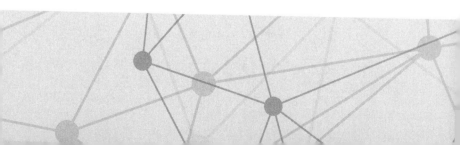

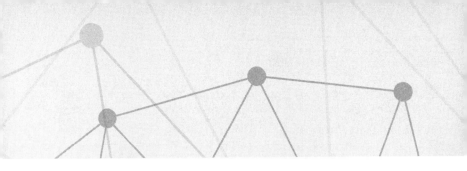

PREFACE

PREFACE

E VERY BUSINESS UNDERSTANDS the critical importance of connecting to its customers. Being close to the customer helps companies establish a conversation and path of discovery that helps drive innovation, thus opening new possibilities and inviting valuable feedback. The very nature of connecting and attracting feedback has long been used to improve products and business offerings for customers.

Think back to the 1950s and the heyday of New York's legendary Madison Avenue "Mad Men" culture. The colossal advertising agencies pushed products through iconic campaigns, such as creating the Marlboro Man to sell cigarettes. These campaigns defined particular personalities and characteristics and suggested a cultural set of preferences, including what you were supposed to wear and look like. Many followed those suggestive and powerful marketing campaigns.

The agency model endures today, though it has been impacted by the arrival of new technologies and ubiquitous access to information. The idea, however, of driving consumers down a single path with communications has gone out of fashion. Today's sophisticated consumers tend to perceive these advertising campaigns as an annoyance with little discernible value.

Our all-digital society leverages an assortment of advanced technologies to reach consumers, penetrate their world, and deliver a persuasive message more effectively. In this new landscape where technology and Millennials are synonymous, poorly conceived and delivered unilateral digital marketing campaigns are viewed as intrusive and impersonal.

The future of digital engagement with consumers demands uniqueness and personalization.

In 2007, Steve Jobs captured the imagination of consumers with Apple's smartphone. This event marked the beginning of a new wave of innovation directed at the end-user market. It also allowed brands to reach the consumer whenever and wherever they were.

Jobs's phenomenon created a new ecosystem of businesses. Many traditional industries looked at this new sensation rocking the marketplace and felt threatened. They rushed to embrace the new digital conversation by conceiving products molded from their Web environment and grafted onto a mobile platform. Most of those efforts generated lackluster products and results. Many businesses mistakenly believed what they had running on the Web would work just as well on a mobile device. They did little or nothing to leverage the native features of the new phones. In essence, there were few results demonstrating an improved experience.

The mobile era was born. It wasn't the first time businesses found themselves behind the curve, desperately trying to catch up to the newest thing.

In this new context, organizations need to embrace technology and unleash their innovation potential in order to transform the future of their business. The concept of "digital" needs to evolve. We are not talking about a new media channel, but rather a foundation to build current and future digital experiences that customers and employees want.

Digital native businesses have discovered ways to establish long-lasting ties with customers by focusing on their experience. We call these turbocharged digital tech companies "disruptors," because they perceived imperfect experiences and made them better. In doing so, these companies shook the very foundation of entire industries and grabbed market share from incumbents. These disrupters, for example, have deeply impacted the industries of music and personal transportation with their digital savvy. What's more, this disruption has spread across every industry and market. It has forced incumbents to come to grips with the reality that they were being disrupted by next-generation players powered by emerging digital technologies infused with design and the ability to scale.

As companies have watched their market share being eroded by digital-savvy companies, they have also suffered losses in talented pools of employees. The new generation of digital workers is being drawn to company cultures driven by powerful digital consumer technologies.

In order for technology to help shape and forge bonds between a brand and its customer or consumers, it requires a commitment on the part of the company to a highly iterative and ongoing evolutionary process. These pools of digital talent will lean toward corporate cultures embracing agile cycles where products are part of an experiential journey. This is the essence of what in this book we are calling the "digital journey."

The demands of the digital marketplace are extremely dynamic and require attention to managing talent, which includes listening to consumers, promoting innovation, and establishing a strong process for the way software is created. This vastly exceeds adopting an agile development process. These are the times in which agility must become enterprise-class.

But to get to the new digital plateau requires rethinking how design, digital technologies, and traditional engineering mesh.

In the early 1980s, when Trip Hawkins founded Electronic Arts (EA), he was credited by analysts and writers with pioneering the concept of treating software as an art form and calling the developers "software artists." EA routinely referred to their developers as "artists" and gave them photo credits in their games and in full-page magazine ads. This novel approach of awarding credit to its developers was one of EA's trademarks in its early days and helped place the company in the limelight of the game industry.

Art was further reinforced into the core of EA's culture and business by packaging most of their games with an "album cover." Hawkins thought that a record album style would both save costs and convey an artistic feeling. The company also shared lavish profits with their developers, which added to their industry appeal. Because of this, EA was easily able to attract the best developers.

These pioneering concepts blazed a new path for innovative software design and approaches, successfully marrying design and innovation with engineering. It is this powerful combination that brings tremendous value to all kinds of software development projects, not just video games. Small teams with cross-functional expertise help drive integration of technology, talent, and ideas, which ultimately drives innovation. But this drive toward forging a union between designers and engineers wasn't a journey without big challenges.

As noted, today's savvy consumers expect well-designed software that's intuitive and delivers a smooth, friction-free experience. Design and simplicity is at the heart of leading-edge software. To get there requires cross-functional expertise.

Software services have come a long way over the past decade. Consumers and business users want digital products that follow them as they pursue a task or seek out information for their needs. The bridging of the two distinctive cultures of art and engineering into an integrated vehicle has helped spur innovation and drive successful projects and engagements with large customer bases.

This first book in a series provides the necessary context, ideas, and selected methodologies that will allow organizations to surf the wave of the digital transformation and help companies bring greater value as they connect with customers and employees in a continuous digital journey.

Having executed thousands of projects for all varieties of organizations, we believe we have distilled here a comprehensive approach to how technology should be developed to achieve success in the digital space.

Trip Hawkins's important insight about the need to bring together art and engineering to design powerful and engaging games now seems obvious to gaming companies. We can only expect that the rich symbiosis of art and engineering for creating all kinds of software will be embraced and seem obvious years from now as the driving force for the digital experience.

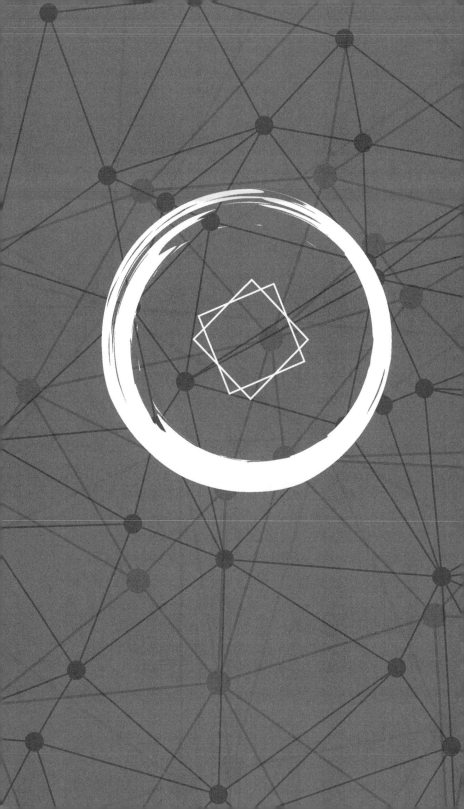

INTRODUCTION
THE DIGITAL JOURNEY

INTRODUCTION
The Digital Journey

I N 2008, A GLOBAL ENTERTAINMENT COMPANY, "M," needed
to improve their client's experience dramatically. M was a
company with a complex structure, including physical and
digital properties, with little or no connection between them.
Their opportunities to cross-sell had been crippled by the lack
of cohesion between business units, which doubled marketing
budgets and overall created a user experience that felt like
talking to disjointed pieces of inconsistent brands.

M wanted to invigorate its websites and create a seamless
experience across the various company units. It wanted to
create a technology blueprint for establishing a coherent
conversation with its customers. The company deeply
understood its customer journey: how customers did research
before a purchase, their main order, their cross-sell purchases,
their service experience, and the follow-up communication and
subsequent purchases. But these channels were disconnected
and weren't digitally integrated. M realized that their designs,
processes, and products that targeted the X and Y generations
were not embracing the digital technologies those consumers

use—and will, increasingly, use in the future. Most of the company's strategies to acquire customers—to get them to buy and keep buying—were campaign-oriented, with heavy traditional marketing budgets for advertising and promotions.

The company's leaders knew they needed a holistic digital product road map, but they were puzzled about how to execute such a strategy, especially given the complexity of the organization and the underlying technology changes, including e-commerce, social media, big data, and mobile and cognitive computing. All these technologies were transforming a consumer's experience, fast. M's executives felt as if the earth was moving underneath them, and they were slipping.

The company's website and mobile apps had become tired compared to more cutting-edge websites, which were rich in video, images, and animation. But most of all, the new digital makeover needed to embrace simplicity in the user experience and be "beautifully" engaging, so that it behaved in a way that anticipated its user's train of thought. In other words, it needed to be a seamless experience that was context-driven, creating a rich, engaging conversation with consumers that would evoke strong emotional responses. The company needed a user interface design that would ensure the experience was smooth and also surprising. M had taken all of these factors into consideration when they created experiences in the physical world for their customers, but that was no longer sufficient, as M was not tackling its next generation of consumers: digital natives.

The company hired a young director, "Joe," who had come over from a major online travel company. He knew that while M's technology culture was mature and its creative talent base was strong, it lacked the digital design and software engineering skills needed to provide the driving force for this big redesign. Joe also knew that the project's success hinged on being able to successfully integrate outside digital software engineers with M's internal technology team, which would be a vexing challenge.

The problem M faced of integrating inside and outside talent is one that plagues many industries and businesses. It's difficult to manage large, complex teams of software engineers, let alone get them to work together—particularly when a company hires an outside firm to work alongside in-house teams. But it's crucial. Twenty years ago, software's use within organizations was limited to companies' corporate process optimization. Now, software underpins nearly every function in every industry and has become critical to survival.

But software development projects are often trouble spots that can lead to failures.

Some of the most common factors underlying software project failures include inaccurate estimates of required resources, inability to handle the project's complexity, unmanaged risks, turf wars, and politics. Engineers and creative design teams often have a difficult time communicating ideas and concepts, and newly minted designs can be fumbled when they are handed over to engineering staff for crafting into products.

A digital focus compels businesses to look internally and assess their technology ecosystems. The trouble is, these ecosystems have a complex array of legacy data and software systems that are difficult to change or modify to meet these new digital requirements. During the past couple of decades, corporations have invested considerably to optimize processes and create efficiencies that changed and modernized their corporate IT infrastructure and services. Many have been very successful. But these technologies fall short in fulfilling the requirements of the digital era, where seamless connectivity between systems serves as the foundation of the digital journeys that consumers and employees expect to experience.

Legacy and core transactional systems comprise old and new technology combined, and in general don't support very frequent releases or continuous delivery; a slower velocity than the development life cycle of digital products. This new technology paradigm requires a two-velocity approach: first, it must meet the requirements of corporate transactional systems, which have traditionally supported the core business and processed critical data; and second, it must allow for a highly iterative, fast cycle of delivery that enables these companies to quickly launch or update new digital products. This is key to enable the digital transformation.

Within large entertainment conglomerates like M, there are distinct divisions that provide experiences to customers across various media. These business units have their own ways of providing experiences and managing brand perception, which are sometimes inconsistent and even conflicting across the company. Just as M acknowledged a problem in the integration of its company at a massive scale, it also realized the tremendous opportunity such an integration would present to leverage scale and connect these experiences in game-changing ways.

M needed a different approach to be digital. This approach was not just about creating more digital products; it was about linking interactions between their products and services within the life of their users. To understand the experience of their users with their products and services, M needed to envision their user journeys in the new digital world.

In simple terms, a digital journey is a context-aware interaction between an end user and a brand or business, whereby the interaction becomes a conversation in which technology facilitates a powerful experience that builds deep emotional connections by incorporating three key values: simplification, surprise, and anticipation.

SIMPLIFICATION is all about minimizing complexity in products, services, or technology yet providing comprehensive functionality.

SURPRISE is at the core of an emotional experience that delights the user yet also helps understand them and their needs with greater precision and predictability.

ANTICIPATION is all about enabling rich connections timed to help the user move forward with their objective, whether that is discovery or completing a tasks or set of tasks.

To create digital journeys, however, requires a confluence of talent, agility, and a corporate culture that promotes innovation, experience design, and technology. M needed a new kind of corporate structure and flexibility to help them integrate their various business units and create an emotionally engaging digital conversation with their customers. They needed a collaborative approach that would permit engineering and design teams to work side by side quickly and efficiently, and at scale, to reach their consumer and business goals.

At the heart of a successful business strategy is a customer experience that is elegantly simple and positive, where consumers are likely to come away satisfied—and return. This type of experience is designed by understanding the emotion of end users throughout a journey involving the company's products and services. The goal is to maximize positive emotion. Ultimately, the goal from the viewpoint of end users' emotional engagement is to elevate a sub-optimal consumer experience into a journey in which the consumers receive high satisfaction.

M had to consider all these issues in redesigning its business within the context of speed. Speed is a central factor when it comes to the execution of a digital strategy; it compels leaders to rethink how software is produced inside and outside of the company. As a business begins to leverage digital and build experiences, software has to be created at a fast pace to leverage multiple channels and entry points. All kinds of devices become components in building and realizing digital journeys.

In today's marketplace, time to market is a chief concern for any business trying to establish or drive digital journeys. Delivering the best experience establishes emotional bonds that last. Arriving late renders a negative impact, a low to no return, and a lackluster effect that lowers brand equity instead of boosting it.

To meet these diverse challenges, teams need to be reworked so that design and engineering work together. What's more, motivational drivers need to be aligned and emphasized to forge a culture of innovation. The challenge was huge for such a large organization. M needed to propel agility and team maturity while implementing a seamless digital journey composed of hundreds of projects, and at the same time integrate in a seamless way design, innovation, and engineering in a single culture—at scale.

And they did great. Today they are one of the most successful digital transformation efforts in the world, and a relevant example that shows big organizations can also be disruptors on the digital arena.

How did they do it?

First, a top-level management decision had to be crafted with a coherent budget. Second, a team had to be assembled that was relevant and well versed in the latest technologies.

Third, a culture needed to be fostered that inspired innovation and allowed employees to explore and imagine these new journeys. Finally, a proper methodology was required to drive and continuously evolve these goals. Out of all these factors, one of the most relevant for the execution was the development methodology that helped M nurture and propel agility and team maturity throughout these digital journeys. This methodology is known as "agile pods." At M, the new manager, Joe, decided to implement its digital transformation by using the agile pods methodology (developed at Globant) and validated in hundreds of digital transformation projects.

Pods are cells comprising designers and engineers with an assortment of digital skills and talents. Typically, a pod has eight to ten team members spanning creative, engineering, and test automation skill sets, all of whom have a shared responsibility for the outcome of a project.

Similar to cells in living organisms, pods have all the equipment and expertise necessary to carry out their functions. They can grow and evolve, maintain the health of the team, and can even replicate themselves. Typically small, they are sometimes part of a larger organism—in this case, a pod ecosystem. As in nature, where there are different kinds of cells, not all pods are equal, and their characteristics will depend on the function to be performed, which may evolve over time. During the development of our agile pods methodology, we stress the importance of multiple pods working seamlessly, as cells in a living organism.

In a large digital transformation initiative, being able to structure an ecosystem of pods brings the scalability, collaboration, and cost-effectiveness any large organization will demand.

This book will focus on the talent, the team structure, the relevant information, and the methodology to carry out a digital transformation.

THE NEVER-ENDING
DIGITAL JOURNEY

Creating new consumer experiences through technology

CHAPTER 1
AGILE ECONOMICS

CHAPTER 1
Agile Economics

HOLLYWOOD IS ALL ABOUT BIG STAKES, whether huge box-office hits or even more colossal failures. When there's a hit, it's astronomical: *Guardians of the Galaxy*, for instance, grossed $332 million with a $170 million budget. But some of the mega box-office failures have been legendary. Recently, the movie *47 Ronin* set a new milestone in gargantuan box-office bombs. The 2013 movie's production budget was $225 million and it earned only $150 million, leaving a $75 million shortfall.

Steep costs and long-term investment cycles have been emblematic of Hollywood's boom-and-bust culture. But there's a new film entertainment model that has emerged over the past few years that is much less risky. In many ways, this new model parallels a new and more cost-effective approach to developing big software projects.

Two of the unlikely pioneers driving this new entertainment model are Netflix and Amazon. Netflix had established itself as a leader in the world of movie distribution and pioneered mailing envelopes for DVDs and streaming movies over the Internet. The behemoth Amazon broke new ground with its new paradigm for online shopping with its recommendation engine. And now both distributors have pivoted in their core businesses and become content creators.

What's new about their approach to films is testing shorter, much less costly pilots to determine which ones have strong audience appeal. By doing so, they can then invest only in those films that are likely to gain traction with viewers and thereby turn a profit. When audiences react against certain storylines, the writers can adjust them, instead of having to forge ahead with characters or subplots that are not resonating with audiences. Now episodes are being created for each story, and they're being measured. This is a closed-loop approach. It's not happening in traditional TV but at the distribution companies. All of the content industry is shifting to this new model.

The many millions of Netflix streaming customers also supply intelligence to the company every time a viewer searches or rates a film negatively or positively. All of it is piped into Netflix's big data stores alongside location data, device data, social media preferences, and bookmarks. That gives the company an abundance of information about its millions of customers' viewing habits and interests. With this rich data approach, neither Netflix nor Amazon have to spend millions just to get people to tune in and view a film.

Netflix became a leader in this new wave of content creators when it released an entire season of episodes of its drama series *House of Cards* at once, giving its customers flexibility in how they viewed it. Netflix executives decided to bankroll the $100 million, two-season series after its subscriber data indicated the popular BBC series, coupled with popular actor Kevin Spacey and director David Fincher, would be a success with its audience.

These testing approaches for creating new content in the entertainment industry parallel what's happening in the software industry. And it's also a less costly and more efficient approach to software development. The investment is smaller and more incremental. Delivering small pieces of a project allows the customer to see what is being produced.

The traditional "waterfall" software development approach embraces a process that begins by defining specifications, then writing code, and then testing the newly produced code. This approach doesn't have the same flexibility of agile development whereby prototypes are built quickly and allow for feedback from customers before the project has consumed weeks or months of time and budget. The waterfall process assumes that functional and technical requirements written at the beginning of a project are a valid approximation of the software products to build. This assumption is seldom true in a context where technology is used to maximize user experience. Waterfall treats change as an exception in the work flow of software development, in a business climate where change is constant. The development team needs to "request" a change of scope to adapt from customer insight or new information. This issue creates a break in the flow, a reestimation of budget and realignment of expectations with stakeholder; that is, time to market is always impacted when changes are required. The lack of agility is a risk that increases exponentially as the digital journeys are more innovative. Maximizing tolerance to change is key to the digital age, which in turn fosters innovation. The loop formed by creation, production, test, and feedback needs to be as short as possible to create the best products; the feedback obtained from users feeds the next phase of design and development and brings digital journeys closer and closer to deliver the desired goals.

After the repetitive and massive failures of the traditional waterfall methodologies, the industry started to move to agile methodologies (what we call "traditional agile methodologies"). In doing so, the gap between what the user was expecting and what the teams were delivering started to shrink. Projects were created in an interactive way, first a minimum viable product and then in short sprints of two or three weeks, releasing new versions of the software each time that more closely fulfilled the needs of the customer. Frequent visualization of the development process revealed the final result was aligned with the original expectations.

Agile methodologies have evolved substantially over the last few years, and have become the de facto standard to deliver digital products. But agile is still not at a level whereby the approach is fully grounded in a set of proven best practices that ensures the success of digital products, either standalone or as part of a journey. Agile is just one piece of the puzzle, and even so, it requires modifications and down-to-earth approaches that take into consideration all of the following realities:

- Designers and engineers need to work together but are seldom aligned by common goals
- Tech talent flocks rapidly from organization to organization; attrition affects retention of core know-how
- Teams are geographically distributed
- Millennials need compatible incentives to become highly productive and innovative, otherwise they will disengage and leave
- Software touches every piece of organizations—its scale can be very large and integration efforts become very complex; hence management of dependencies among teams has become critical to ensure successful delivery
- In most cases, agile teams are recognized by their companies as an investment in future capital; hence methodologies need to have cost efficiency and return built into their processes and metrics

During the creation of digital journeys, companies need to be capable of overcoming the following challenges:

- Talent (internal and external) needs to evolve to better understand and hence connect with customers so their digital journeys are continuously enhanced. To do so requires team members to grow their talent base, regardless of their technology experience. In doing so, they help build value into the consumer experience and consequently gain deeper insights into the business domain. It's critical to retain core talent. Motivation, engagement, and drive are of utmost importance for the long-term success of digital strategies.

- Experience design is at the core of generating digital journeys, which means designers and engineers need to learn to collaborate in this culture of innovation.

- As the digital program scales and more products become part of the customer experience, new solutions will emerge, new innovative journeys will be created, alongside existing journeys being evolved. At this stage, the program needs to leverage economies of scale. It should be cheaper to create innovative journeys and evolve existing ones as the digital organization matures.

Generic agile methodologies are not comprehensive enough to solve for all of the challenges businesses today face on their quest to become digital.

The economic implications of using agile methodologies in software development are considerable. Like one-hour TV episodes, shorter-scope software coding projects can be undertaken without locking the product owner into long, fixed-price contracts for several months of development. This is especially relevant when a company has contracted an outside software vendor to provide development services. As new prototypes are built and tested with real users, there is greater accountability, as users can experience and provide feedback before making a sizable and costly investment into a long-term software development project.

A few years ago, the retail movie rental business Blockbuster closed its last few hundred stores. The company's dramatic fall from industry leader to bankruptcy has become a classic case study referenced in business schools and boardrooms. The company failed to adapt its business model as the market changed to online streaming. Similarly, new models of movie production are challenging the incumbent entertainment giants with nimble, lower-risk and cost approaches to producing successful television shows. And the software industry is also facing big challenges in the dynamic marketplace, where customers are looking for innovative, consumer-friendly software produced faster, more efficiently, and at lower cost. Those that adapt are more likely to survive and flourish than those that hold on to outdated models.

CHAPTER 2
WHAT'S WRONG
WITH SOFTWARE

CHAPTER 2
What's Wrong with Software

I N THE WORLD OF DIGITAL MEDIA, consumer expectations
have changed dramatically. After a few decades of Internet
shopping, reading, watching videos, and searching for product
information and opinions, people have high expectations
for a seamless, simple, digital journey experience. And
when they don't find what they're looking for in easy and
fluid interactions, they complain using the megaphone of
social media, or simply do not adopt the product and move
elsewhere in the digital world, thus impacting brand equity.
Companies realize the stakes for software development have
increased exponentially.

We are living in amazing times for software—many of the
applications we're using didn't exist five or six years ago. And
we've become used to beautifully designed applications on our
mobile phones that combine big-data components and gaming
behaviors. The truth is, we are now used to these applications,
which didn't exist before, and many businesses and entire
industries are lagging in terms of making the experience
sufficiently engaging to avoid an eventual disruption by a digital

native (person or company born in the digital era that embraces lean, leading-edge technologies) that changes the game.

The generation of new devices including smartphones and tablets are so easy and intuitive to navigate that children are able to shop, surf, and interact on these devices without any training. In this brave new world of instant access and fulfillment, companies can't afford to be left behind and risk losing their ability to both attract and hold onto customers who don't have an ideal user experience.

These technological shifts are affecting the role of design in business, approaches to globalization, the triple bottom line (an accounting framework comprised of three parts: social, environmental, and financial), and the overarching realization that innovation drives business and design enables innovation. What's more, environmental responsibility and universal design were once an option; now they are becoming a mandate. Experience design, interaction design, and service design are current domains for designers with the emphasis on "the future is now."

Businesses are driven to create cutting-edge, consumer-facing digital technologies by necessity. They also crave doing so because it's an opportunity to engage in a continuous conversation with their customers, interact, and leverage the right technology to understand, analyze, predict, suggest, and convert customers.

This digital engagement is important to young companies, but even more so to global companies with decades of market history, experience, and brand awareness. These industry behemoths possess an enormous amount of content and understand their customers. But many find themselves frustrated that they can't express any of this great information in touch-points to their customers because they don't have the digital design and functions in place to drive this new, all-digital conversation.

Companies have been struggling to keep up with this wave of dramatic digital changes. To adapt to these shifts, some corporations have acquired innovative software technology companies to help them blaze a new path. Others have pursued a combination of technology assets and talented "rock star" software developers to catalyze and drive innovation from within. Unfortunately, only a few of these strategies have proved successful and sustainable in harnessing new digital technologies that help drive home corporate brand value to customers.

Large companies are trying to reinvent themselves in this all-new digital era. Companies are aware of the huge long-term stakes, and have established new executive management positions, such as the Chief Digital Officer, to address the challenges. That position has been created to drive new digital initiatives that span the entire corporation and its business units. This in itself has also created new friction within executive management as the new roles and responsibilities of the Chief Digital Officer have overlapped with the Chief Information Officer. To add further complexity, the Chief

Marketing Officer's position has evolved to embrace more technology-savvy responsibilities and has progressively taken budget control and accountability from the CIO. These top-level shifts and changes will need sorting out to ensure greater efficiency. Until the right person is placed in command, there will certainly be greater tension over control rather than focus on solutions that address the central needs for highly innovative software products.

Software has become the common denominator for every type of business, nearly every function in every industry, and has become critical for almost every company's bottom line. So it's not surprising that software development projects are often trouble spots that can lead to failures.

Worldwide, it's hard to say how many software projects fail or how much money is wasted as a result. If you define failure as the total abandonment of a project before or shortly after it is delivered, and if you accept a conservative failure rate of 5 percent, then billions of dollars are wasted each year on bad software. With a lack of accurate metrics to reveal the actual failure rate, the software industry recognizes software projects fail (or partially fail) at a rate of 30 percent to 50 percent.

This new all-digital era, where low-cost global communications are enriched by the Internet, has forever reduced the expense and difficulty of coordinating the work of global teams in faraway locations. Still, the dream concept of handing off tasks that "follow the sun" and leverage twenty-four-seven software development cycles has never been fully realized because of big challenges involving communication gaps, complexity, management, quality, etc.

It's important for companies to identify the underlying factors that are responsible for most software project failures. Many have to do with a lack of coordination of resources on many levels—time, money, communication between design and engineering and other teams.

Often, companies experience what is called the "let's not work together syndrome." This is when product design and engineering efforts are out of sync. These are two critical pieces of equal importance in the software development life cycle, but often they are at odds, whether because of timing, priorities, or goals.

One of the problems with many software development projects is an over-focus on defining the process, the technology, and the projects, and doing too little developing a quick feedback loop that includes end users. With this loop in place, there's a way to evolve the features to impress and engage users, which translates to value. Companies spend a great deal of time mocking up and defining road maps, requirements, and journeys for software—often scrapping whole pieces when they don't work out—instead of creating working prototypes that evolve through testing and user feedback. Trying to design software from these sorts of prefabbed specifications discourages discovery and innovation because these deliverables seldom meet the real end user soon enough to validate the assumptions made by the business, product, or technology teams.

Another issue many companies face, particularly big ones, is having too many moving parts operating toward different and, in many cases, mismatched goals. A software project road map may be implemented through multiple divisions, third parties, agencies, and contractors, creating a potential nightmare of communication mishaps and timing problems. Too often, one part is waiting on another—or worse, has the wrong idea of what the other part is working on or when it is going to deliver. It feels as though, as developers, we feel safer confining ourselves to our own controlled environments, where we perceive a fake stability, teams make individual, siloed progress, and get farther and farther away from the common goals for the product or technology envisioned. Thus, at integration points, when the silos are forced to come together, we blame external factors (including other teams) instead of looking introspectively and facing the reality that, at scale, we don't know how to handle effective communication among teams, and we don't know how to "goal" teams for collaboration. We may also assume that a conflicting governance model where product, design, and technology work under incompatible goals will deliver the vision.

The lack of timing coordination leads to "inventing the schedule." All the various components of a software development team estimate their needs for time and resources based on murky, unchecked assumptions, which means that costs and time can go spiraling out of control and completely derail a budget and schedule estimates.

Meanwhile, in this era when engineers are so highly sought after, some talent becomes a bit too demanding. There's the "software is a craft" myth, where developers can act like rock stars and underestimate metrics and projections based on productivity results. Companies aren't making handcrafted pickles in a barrel in Brooklyn; they're creating software, which can be measured and predicted effectively. To perform accurate estimates on software development implies continuous refinement. But in reality, it's more likely that it's not until after the initial ideation and prototyping stages have been completed, when production of the software becomes more predictable and measurable. What this means is that the key to fostering innovation requires measuring progress, adjusting, and requesting higher velocity from the teams as designs and dependencies to content and platform are known. The vision for the digital journey is established at ideation and requires that design disciplines be interwoven into the life cycle of software development.

The notion of "design thinking," at its most abstract, was deftly handled by Tim Brown in his book *Change by Design: How Design Thinking Transforms Organizations and Inspires Innovation*. Brown frames the idea of design thinking around an approach that says, "Design thinking starts with divergence, the deliberate attempt to expand the range of options rather than narrow them…. To harvest the power of design thinking, individuals, teams, and whole organizations have to cultivate optimism. People have to believe that it is within their power (or at least the power of their team) to create new ideas that will serve unmet needs and that will have a positive impact."

The concepts of design thinking are also embraced and applied to the notion that business culture and design are interdependent in Thomas Lockwood's book, *Design Thinking: Integrating Innovation, Customer Experience, and Brand Value.* He postulates that all parts of a process need to be interwoven. The challenge of driving innovative and thoughtful design for digital applications requires effort and an awareness that integration is crucial to success. "Embedding design requires unique processes," he writes, "yet these processes need to be integrated with other key business processes, or they won't get traction."

In his book, Lockwood outlines seven simple steps to integrate design into corporate culture.

1. Determine cultural norms and drivers
2. Determine how design can support the norms
3. Build awareness about the value of design
4. Set appropriate design organization and partners
5. Integrate design processes within corporate business policies and practices
6. Measure the value gained by design
7. Train and empower others in design thinking methods

Software creation, in this view, is an inherently team-based process. Knowing this, large and small software companies can build teamwork into their ethos. Teams assemble and reassemble based on specific projects. Companies depend on core organizational elements and structures to help make the collaboration work.

Storytelling is deeply linked into the process by which teams drive a company's digital journey. In *Change by Design*, Tim Brown emphasizes the importance of storytelling and its relationship to design thinking. "Mostly we rely on stories to put our ideas into context and give them meaning," Brown writes. "It should be no surprise, then, that the human capacity for storytelling plays an important role in the intrinsically human-centered approach to problem-solving, design thinking."

In the midst of this sea change of creativity and digital design, a core concept for creating viable digital journeys is the ideation process. It is here where validation takes place in a dynamic, interdependent linkage between the ideation and prove phases, which are tightly coupled to the execution of the overall building process. In simple terms, the ideation phase is inextricably connected to the prove phase, much like a biofeedback loop for a living organism, where the high-frequency cycling of digital nutrients generates catalytic innovation enzymes that drives the digital journey forward (see diagram "The Never-Ending Digital Journey," Chapter 4). This concept is fundamental when it comes to building consumer software.

In these types of applications, understanding the reaction of the consumer after a prototype (Minimal Viable Product) is released is critical. It also makes possible the downstream iterative steps where the concepts change and evolve based on lessons learned from consumers, who in many ways form a virtual focus group. The ultimate validation for software is when the application goes into action and we can see it working: "We don't believe it until we see it."

CHAPTER 3
WHAT IS DIGITAL SUCCESS

CHAPTER 3
What is Digital Success

T HE GLOBAL WEB OF ECONOMIC interconnections between countries and companies is being driven by digital technologies and is growing larger, stronger, and more complex by the day. A broad array of emerging technologies is being embraced to help convert physical experiences of customers into virtual ones that emotionally connect to them and shape companies' digital journeys.

This transformation is not only happening for customers, it's also happening inside companies as digital progress touches nearly every part of an organization, which means any large digital programs require unprecedented coordination of people, processes, and technologies. Digital success for the corporation implies higher returns as products with better engagement are realized and better productivity and innovation are maintained in concert with motivated employees.

A strategy to increase revenue from high-value customer segments, for example, requires analytics-based insights to determine a clear vision and plan for how to capture the most value from the digital transformation. New capabilities and teams are also needed to manage and coordinate the delivery of those digital journeys across the organization.

The factors that influence digital success are as follows:

TOP MANAGEMENT ALIGNMENT: Any transformational program requires the support and sponsorship of management in order to be successful. An organic approach is preferred to re-org, whereby new leadership is identified to drive new strategic digital initiatives. This kind of reordering of management has implications for any business, and can be disruptive. Companies that have successfully transformed their businesses followed a management path that mirrored the iterative digital journey, which is horizontal in its approach. Enabling digital journeys requires coordination from multiples divisions and departments. The transformation starts by sharing common goals instilled from the top and consistent to the bottom of the organization.

BUDGET TO FIXED CORE CAPACITY: The digital program, as it achieves scale, requires budget flexibility to expand, contract capacity, and make agile turns in its strategy as it's gathering insight from its users, competition, and as business evolves. As opposed to traditional IT, where projects need to be approved on a case-by-case basis, creating digital journeys needs to be approved in time boxes. These are called waves (see Chapter 4). Using this approach, a new time box gets infused with cash and will be approved as key performance metrics pass the minimum criteria. These KPI are data points defined by the business, such as: the number of new clients, the size of revenues through digital channels, the percentage increase in customer retention, and the percentage productivity increase in customer support functions. (See Chapter 6, The Power of Metrics)

CULTURE: A culture of innovation is nurtured and grown by strengthening the DNA and incentivizing digital product incumbents to join the innovation wave instead of being left outside of and becoming suspicious of it. Division owners, managers, and leaders need to feel incentivized and eager to grasp the opportunities for change; their importance needs to be explained eloquently by top management, and their compensation and career path needs to be consistently influenced by the results of the transformation. Alongside the importance of proper alignment, there are proven practices in order to foster a new, stronger digital culture, all of which require education and ongoing coaching. Training is approached pragmatically, with real-world cases in which all training content is both proven and credible. Coaching is an ongoing activity and the job of leaders in any digital transformational program. Those leaders need to be recognized as such by large portions of the organization.

PLATFORMS: Successful digital journeys are enabled by the underlying software architecture upon which they're built, with integrated digital technologies products and services.

Most businesses' technology infrastructure is characterized by a mix of modern and legacy technology comprising disparate, disconnected hardware and software silos. There is a considerable challenge in how to design and implement the optimal way to access data swiftly in an environment of different mobile and desktop devices with the goal of creating a seamless experience for the end user. Moreover, the challenge doesn't end with internal systems, because businesses need to leverage data outside of the company's firewalls to better understand the consumer's tendencies. Further compounding the challenge is that businesses are implementing different execution strategies as they pursue their digital journey, and this leads to ongoing change. Helping make these disparate systems connect and communicate requires rewriting software for back-end legacy systems, which is prohibitively expensive. The solution involves the creation of software services that run over existing platforms, thus becoming bridges across vertical silos within business units, divisions, and channels. These platforms are defined as an open, "micro-services" architecture that "glues" the various pieces of the puzzle. As internal data are processed, external data simultaneously enters the data ecosystem. That data is processed through business rules, heuristics, or machine learning algorithms that look for correlations and patterns. These findings relate to user behavior and how it impacts their profile, preferences, and moods. These services run over a variety of different hardware and software platforms and ultimately help enrich each consumer's digital journey. In doing so, they pave the way for incremental success, which feeds long-term digital transformation efforts.

The factors outlined above are required to drive digital success, but central to them is the talent that makes all of this happen. And talent needs to be cultivated—incentivized so that it evolves in alignment with business objectives and motivates employees to stay and progressively improve their level of expertise. With those elements in place, innovation flourishes and employees are excited to push boundaries and deliver superior digital journeys. These dynamics are set into motion by pods that drive and optimize the digital transformation process for successful outcomes.

Pods are cells comprising designers and engineers with an assortment of digital skills and talents. Typically, a pod has eight to ten team members spanning creative, engineering, and test automation skill sets. Pods can be cells composed of in-house talent (internal pods), and there can also be pods composed of talent from partners or vendors (external pods). All pods form an "ecosystem"—they will depend on each other for assets, components, or information. So, regardless of company, divisional, or political boundaries, the "ecosystem" has same top-level goals, which are shared by all pods.

Pods can be measured and monitored continuously. In any software development vendor relationship, this fact stands in sharp contrast to a fixed-price engagement, where every time the scope changes it impacts the overall cost of the engagement. Moreover, the pod methodology allows for an incremental development process by which aspects of functionality can be tested to determine if the project needs to pivot before producing other software components. Another benefit to this stepwise approach is that it helps align incentives with the total cost of ownership. As the project progresses, efficiencies are gained and the pod is incentivized to be more productive or create new products. With external pods, this methodology helps to reassure the customer (who has internal and external pods) that the fees paid to external pods are optimal. That is: the overall cost of ownership is reduced as the cost of pods goes up, because the pod cannot increase its cost without proving a productivity, quality, or combined improvement that surpasses the cost increase. This cost model (a.k.a. maturity) is further explained in Chapter 4: "How Pods Deliver Digital Transformation" and Chapter 6: "The Power of Metrics."

As pod teams move further along in the software development project, competition also helps drive the teams to create strong products that meet the customer's needs in an efficient manner.

Pods are execution-focused in that they are used to build, evolve prototypes, and create products employing innovative trends and technology. Pods approach projects with combined art and science. Art lives in the content and science lives in the execution. When a company embarks on a journey, executing a digital road map, this vision evolves throughout the pod-driven process.

The structure and methodology that accompany pods ensures companies receive not only robust design, innovation, and engineering teams, but also ones that are integrated and work together seamlessly and intuitively—almost like a biological system. This team—or "pod"—can create its own kind of ecosystem, which is balanced, sustainable, and replicable.

Pods incorporate a diverse set of proven concepts and methodologies, including organizational dynamics, psychology, and game design. They were designed with the express purpose of helping organizations and companies overcome the huge barriers and challenges they face when trying to create, manage, and build digital journeys. By offering real-time monitoring and management functions, the pods' tools and methodologies help companies improve the overall productivity of developer teams by establishing richer flow between them.

Also, pods help companies overcome long wait times. When various team members are waiting on each other to complete a part of the project, companies encounter cost overruns—and frustrations. But with an integrated pod ecosystem, team members can work on various aspects of the project without blocking themselves. The process by which an ecosystem unblocks itself at scale is called "rebalancing."

At its most fundamental unit, the pod is designed as an

inherently balanced team that evolves the way an organism does when faced with challenges or adversity. It permits companies to track their teams and supplement them with needed resources. And it gives organizations better control over the outcomes and costs of development project work. As a pod matures, it forges innovation DNA that can then be used as starter material to generate a new pod. In keeping with the dynamics of a living cell, the division of a pod is much like its biological counterpart, called mitosis.

But pods are not just a group of people—rather, they are interconnected to other pods and groups, whereby they gain the ability to scale, which is by design inherently organic. The critical developmental path emerges in much the same way a neural network changes when new inputs are made available. Pods enable companies to create an underlying structure to coordinate disparate parts—design, engineering, management, product, finance, customer insights, and technology infrastructure.

Built into the function of pods is their ability to operate with a "fail fast" approach within key phases of the Digital Evolution Life Cycle (see Chapter 4). With better communication and integration, the pods can iterate fast, without waiting on one another. That helps eliminate one of the main causes of failure in most large-scale software projects, where one team member or group of developers has to wait on another developer or team. The integrated mesh of pods solves this problem by virtue of its "pod ecosystem" dynamics.

Adaptability is central to all aspects of pods and their life cycle. It is pods' ability to adapt and morph quickly that helps delineate an optimal working path. These capabilities help businesses realize and settle on the outcome of the synergistic "ideation and prove" stages that deliver a successful minimally viable product (MVP) faster in the journey. Once this critical step is achieved, the technology can be scaled to realize the benefits of the digital transformation. This "fast cycling" of ideation and prove is reflected in the software development cycles being shorter, as products try and fail fast. Once the MVP has wings, the approach is to adapt quickly to consumers and to continue following this path in a never-ending cycle of innovation and return. The overall aim is similar to the new movie business, where a film studio like Netflix produces a successful multiseason hit series through the iterative process of adapt, surprise, engage, retain, and monetize. This approach applies equally to journeys involving digital products targeting consumers or employees.

Companies that have embraced the pod model have realized an average net savings of 30 percent developing software, stemming from more successful minimum viable products (MVP), minimized rework, higher autonomy, velocity, and further efficiencies. What's more, those companies have also been able to monitor the productivity of their software teams and create incentives that retain talent, which otherwise can be flighty. Talented engineers aren't loyal unless they're engaged. Pods work within a goal strategy that combines "what's in it" for each actor in the entire ecosystem, which helps steer the digital transformation to success.

CHAPTER 4

HOW PODS DELIVER
DIGITAL TRANSFORMATION

CHAPTER 4
How Pods Deliver Digital Transformation

I N THE FALL OF 2013, UK newspapers carried stories of a massive technology debacle involving the government's National Health Service (NHS), which had scrapped a patient record system costing taxpayers £10 billion. Over nearly ten years, the government software project, the National Programme for IT, had involved many large contractors working on various parts of a complex system, which ultimately failed due to poor management and coordination, and a failure to understand or communicate with the people who were supposed to use the system. Newspapers and analysts agreed that, as the *Guardian* put it, this was "the biggest IT failure ever seen."

The project was launched in 2002 with the ambitious aim of revolutionizing better healthcare delivery with new technologies, which included electronics records, digital scanning, and integrated IT systems across hospitals and community care operations. But the effort was beset by many problems, including changing specifications for the technology and disputes with suppliers, which ultimately left the project years behind schedule and over budget. Throughout the project's life, key stakeholders within the health system, such as doctors, expressed concern about the accessibility and utility of the planned system. Eventually, Parliament reviewed the National Programme for IT and decided to dismantle the project.

The colossal problems that plagued the NHS are ones that many large-scale software development projects in corporations, organizations, and governments are familiar with, often with similarly fateful and costly outcomes. The software was developed without input or metrics about what users needed, an approach that is destined for these kinds of complications. The longstanding software development approach as discussed earlier has been framed around writing specifications and then doing the software coding, followed by testing and delivering it to the users. At the end of the process, what gets delivered is often not what the customer wants.

At the heart of the NHS project's problem was the way it was structured and designed. The project involved multiple government contractors, whose capabilities were assessed with various methodologies used by the government. When there are so many contractors involved and an unclear, overarching process to develop the software, the overall architecture is designed on top of a mountain of assumptions. Requests for Proposals (RFP) are sent out, formal responses are obtained, and there's nothing that prevents a well-qualified vendor from being awarded the project contract without actually proving, with an actual team, that they will be able to execute, sync up with the rest of the moving parts, and complete the scope of work successfully. An RFP ends in a multiplicity of negotiations whereby each vendor gets a piece of the pie, some much more than others. Innovation and expertise often loses out to a vendor's political clout and ability to secure the deal. Vendors can appear competent when they showcase official certifications by accredited institutions. But all too often, politics becomes the deciding factor, instead of a rigorous and systematic approach that can be objectively monitored with data that shows whether the project was successful or not.

One of the common certifications widely embraced in the software industry is the Capability Maturity Model (CMM), a formal development model created several years ago to help objectively assess the ability of software companies to implement a project. CMM comprises a five-point scale that defines and scores a software development project from low to high optimization. The underlying logic of the CMM is that it guides a project, both in terms of time and budget, with the objective of improving CMM levels of maturity to the most optimized level (see Glossary).

The CMM model employs the word "maturity" to describe and quantify the degree of optimization of software development processes. It provides a theoretical continuum along which a series of maturity stages incrementally move from one level to the next. Each maturity level is characterized by five key factors: goals, commitment, ability, measurement, and verification.

Pods also employ the concept of maturity in the model.

But unlike CMM, the standard parameters pods measure are velocity, quality, autonomy, and other criteria, which are customized to the specifics of each digital journey (see Chapter 6, "The Power of Metrics"). These different dimensions of maturity can be constructed from basic metrics and calculated in near real time. This places the pods in a maturity path whereby the progress can be measured alongside the actual value delivered in a project, which also incorporates an incentive system that establishes a career path for pod members.

In pods, the concept of maturity is holistic, looking at the entire team (or teams) involved in making or sustaining software products. This method can be supported by tools, like GoPods (see Afterword), that help managers and executives visualize all elements in the software development ecosystem, including the products or components being built, leveraging and optimizing existing software development management tools. The basic underlying premise here is not to "reinvent the wheel," but to have a holistic viewpoint and an ability for a manager to analyze scenarios at various granularities of pod levels—project and ecosystem (several pods addressing different aspects of the digital road map)—and then make changes dynamically. The ability to have a centralized view with zoom-in and -out capability yielding more granular resolution of these integrated processes provides managers with a more intuitive and easy-to-understand tool so they can take the right corrective action to improve efficiency or address a problem.

Maturity is a core component in the structure, function, and overall efficiency of pods. Each pod is assigned a maturity level. The maturity level is a combination of metrics that are weighted and aligned with business plan goals, such as time to market, quality, killer feature impact, and cost efficiency. When pods attain a higher level of maturity, the company rewards its members with monetary incentives, such as higher compensation or a special bonus, or nonmonetary incentives, such as an assignment to more visible projects or exposure to cutting-edge, emerging technologies that translates into status and recognition across the organization. If a pod doesn't attain a higher maturity level, there is no penalty to the pod members. However, the systematic performance stagnation or decline will eventually trigger an action called a "rebalancing in the pod(s)." Some of the possible outcomes from this rebalancing could include, pods being split, augmented, or members could change roles or be removed from the road map. The rebalancing will effectively be triggered as a function of how the malfunctioning pod affects the critical path and compromises business goals (see "Agile Pod Principles" chart, opposite).

Both pods and the surrounding ecosystem are agile. The old software development paradigm of defining, building, and testing is history. Today, companies of all shapes and sizes need to be much more dynamic and more oriented to customer feedback. This is the new scenario.

"Innovation requires having at least three things: a great

idea, the engineering talent to execute it, and the business savvy (plus deal-making moxie) to turn it into a successful product," writes Walter Isaacson in his book, *The Innovators: How a Group of Hackers, Geniuses, and Geeks Created the Digital Revolution.*

AGILE POD PRINCIPLES

VISION ALIGNMENT
From inception a pod begins aligning goals for all parties involved: employees, business, partners

Employee benefits: *A pod has better exposure to best projects and a higher basic compensation. Attaining a higher maturity incentivizes pod members with financial and nonfinancial compensation.*

Partner benefits: *vendors and partners are incentivized to achieve maturity. A bonus over maturity levels or a percentage increase is negotiated, which makes partners willing to invest to encourage maturity.*

Businesses benefits: *a higher maturity level brings additional performance, which is incrementally higher than its cost. Additional performance at expected or superior quality improve time to market. Also, business can define maturity criteria to incentivize partners or vendors to include maturity metrics, which are directly related to their digital journey performance, particularly defining metrics such as customer acquisition, retention, conversion, savings, etc.*

Mitosis

Like a living cell, propagates pod's DNA to help scale and improve overall ecosystem performance

Benefits: *Scalability, knowledge propagation, learning curves*

Maturity Path

Aligns pod members' goals to business results with a variety of rewards (financial, status, and recognition)

Benefits: *Motivation, autonomy, high performance, innovation*

Autonomy

Tech and business domain knowledge and experience grows, helping drive delegation

Benefits: *Maximized agility and efficiency, better time to market, critical path always visible, organic synergy*

Collaboration

Common sense of purpose given by clarity in their interdependencies and position within the pod ecosystem

Benefits: *Maximize the flow of work, minimizing dependency or talent defienciency bottlenecks*

Transparency

Metrics provide an objective way to ascertain and track progress and results. Traceable and simple to understand metrics, incentives reinforce optimal behavior for desired outcomes.

Benefits: *Real-time critical path, predictability on quality, time to market, and lower cost of digital strategy*

Both pods and their individual members are rated and rewarded for their maturity levels. The first goal for a new pod member is to gain status as a core member, which allows him or her much greater flexibility in moving to other pods within the company. During the course of a project, shorter-term goals are set and awarded to individuals to maintain their motivation until they meet the requirements. It is like a game, wherein its members become part of a guild with a common mission.

This project mission gets aligned with the overall business goals, such as time to market, quality, and a better innovative user experience. Each project weighs the biases of its own set of goals and prioritizes the most important. This becomes the basis for what is termed the minimum viable product (MVP). For example, building a mobile GPS navigation system requires a diversity of inputs, such as traffic information, quality and user interface design, and an overall user experience, all of which are critical to the product's adoption. In addition to the basic elements of a quality GPS navigation system, for example, the team would need to add an edge—a set of social functions that differentiated the product by allowing users to send and receive events in real time, based on things happening on the road. This addition became the innovative feature. With that understanding, the goals for pods working on the project were established with the emphasis on innovation around socializing traffic events and improved user interface design goals, while velocity became a secondary goal.

Once the basic features were discovered, prototyped, and proven with some users, the pod's goal shifted toward velocity. That meant that the metrics of the maturity of the pods subsequently became heavily driven by productivity and quality. The maturity criteria help drive the ecosystem's focus on what matters most to the business and what will ultimately make the product successful in the market.

This approach sharply contrasts other software development models, which prioritize structure and standards. Pods drive the software development process, which also improves and morphs talent and skill sets of the pod members. In an economy of software innovation, pods are able to efficiently adapt to the challenge because they are designed to evolve as the digital journey is better understood. This understanding also permits the free flow of end customers' insights, which are continuously integrated into the development life cycle.

A critical underpinning for successful innovations is a dynamic and balanced ecosystem. Pods forge an ecosystem for the express purpose of driving innovation (see "Agile Pods Ecosystem" diagram opposite).

THE AGILE POD ECOSYSTEM

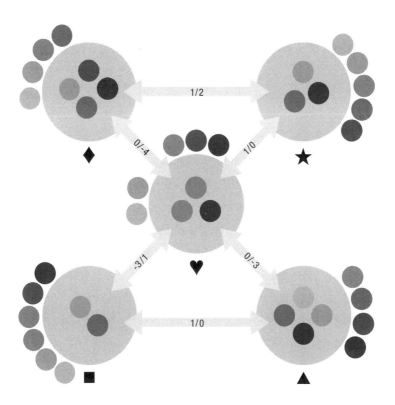

This graph shows a pod ecosystem, its interdependencies, and the flow of communication that takes place.

The dots inside the circle are core members, and the external dots represent pod members, with varying talents that "extend" the core.

The arrows show the dependencies among pods. For example, Square owes at least one component to Triangle today; Triangle is delayed, as it shows a -3 days overdue.

The ability to see real-time dependencies helps to determine the critical path for each digital journey. The critical path allows pod leaders to rebalance the pod ecosystem to attain higher velocity, better quality, and a lower cost per point, all of which depends upon the prevailing business goal and stage of the digital evolution life cycle (see Chapter 4).

The importance of an ecosystem to innovation is the central thesis of Ron Adner's book, *The Wide Lens: A New Strategy for Innovation*. Adner, a professor at Dartmouth's Tuck Business School, cites several examples where innovations failed and how success in a connected world requires management of one's dependence. One of the classic innovation failures that Adner cites looks back to the 1990s, when Michelin developed a revolutionary new kind of tire with sensors and an internal hard wheel that could run almost perfectly for 125 miles after a puncture. A light on the dashboard would notify the driver of a puncture, which would permit the driver to deal with the problem when it was convenient. Customers would benefit from greater safety and Michelin would make money. Powerful partnerships were assembled with Audi, Goodyear, Honda, and Mercedes. But by 2007, the product was such a failure that Michelin abandoned it.

What Michelin failed to grasp was the entire ecosystem its product would rely upon, such as garages to repair punctured tires. Those smaller garages would need to buy and house the new equipment to support the new product. And they didn't buy into it.

Another hi-tech example is Sony's failure to grapple with the whole ecosystem when it rolled out its reader for e-books in 2007. It overlooked the economic and legal issues around digital rights management solution and fell flat building a compelling online store.

What Adner drives at in his book is the idea that success requires the innovator to recognize they're part of a larger innovation ecosystem. And without being able to see the larger context, an innovative software development effort, for example, will most likely fail. A pod ecosystem that is continually being rebalanced is required to build innovative products.

Now the key follow-up question: how do these digital products coexist and fulfill an experience, increase the level of engagement, and support the business to create a long-lasting emotional link with consumers or employees through technology?

Many businesses have repurposed their websites in an effort to build customer engagement through mobile devices with applications that reach their consumers or employees in a convenient, intuitive way. Most companies, however, have not leveraged the innate characteristics of mobile devices and build nonintuitive apps that consumers do not embrace.

The root cause can often be traced back to the "ideation stage" (design stage) of these apps, when the development process lacked the conceptual framework of establishing a digital journey or experience for the consumer (see "The Never-Ending Journey" diagram that follows). That entails creating a cohesive context and pathway for how the consumer interacts with a product or service and makes decisions at various stages of the process. During this kind of interaction, where a user embraces a product or service, the technology establishes a powerful experience that forges deep emotional connections with the key elements of simplification, surprise, and anticipation. This emphasis and focus, however, does not fit within today's traditional software development regimen in companies that have not been born to produce digital products.

With pods, the ideation phase generates the foundation and building blocks from which digital journeys are shaped. Pods supply the talent sources that design and prove journeys. Those journeys can then be scaled and evolved in an efficient and continuous way that refines and innovates the user experience.

THE NEVER-ENDING DIGITAL JOURNEY

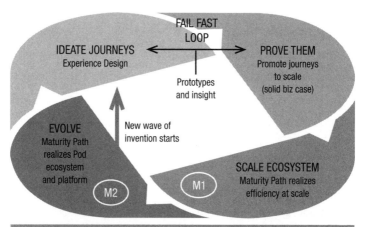

The foundation for all digital journeys is a virtual life cycle. The process begins in ideation (design) phase when ideas are formulated, iterated, and assessed to high-potential prototypes.

Pods are created at all phases of the cycle: at the initial "ideation stage," or during the later stages, when the project has grown significantly and reached scale. The ideation stage consists primarily of defining the digital journey with the product owners, "dreaming" the employee experience. In effect, the goal of this phase is to create a 10,000-foot view for the products in the journey, including a road map and target customers, which are rigorously defined with emotional cues (highs and lows) that traverse and enrich the customer's experience.

This process emphasizes discovery and also allows product owners, designers, and engineers the opportunity to collaborate and synergize on better ways to engage while enhancing the consumer's overall experience. This digital engagement may take shape through products or services that a company sells, or it might happen between employees and their interactions with corporate technology.

The journey is conceptualized using cinematic techniques, video productions, and physical props. This approach differs greatly from traditional software design and development, which relies solely on text and graphs to showcase experiences and describe scenarios.

Once the pods are established and set into motion, they morph as more information is gathered about the products, its users, and the environment in which they are being designed to operate, i.e. their ecosystem is rebalanced as these assumptions become "proven." The pods' success always hinges on a fail-fast cycle of successful prototypes (the ideation-prove becomes a fast iteration cycle interacting with relevant users: employees and/or consumers).

This typically takes shape when the initial solution pods (design, project management, or development pods) split, via a division similar to mitosis, to form a fast-prototyping ecosystem. What's important to note here is that as the pods mature, so does the environment that surrounds it, forging a solutions backbone realized by the higher maturity pods (core pods). In simple terms, solution and development pods are required as the capacity need grows to accommodate the need for more development skills to further design.

The solution pods are continuously sent feedback, and throughout the process, pods grow in maturity as they understand more about the journey and the desired products.

At scale (see "The Never-Ending Digital Journey" diagram on previous pages), when several pods are working in this coordinated fashion within an ecosystem, all of the pods take on various roles of responsibility and have different levels of maturity.

For example, **Solution Pods** will have higher maturity levels and take on the responsibility to propel innovation and realize the objectives for the particular technology or product road map.

Development Pods will focus on developing new features and organizing the overall process so that it delivers production-ready code.

Evolution Pods are designed to improve features and functions alongside design and technical requirements on working products.

DevOps Pods are designed to measure, monitor, and run

the digital ecosystem among the various channels. This also involves listening to client feedback and then interacting with the ecosystem to ensure the audience is heard.

In summary, the pods are still united by the same goals, values, customer adoption objectives, and retention, as well as time to market and monetization. They ideate and go through this fail-fast cycle. The various types of pods come together as the journeys achieve **scale** (i.e., as they pass from a high-frequency iterative **ideation-prove** phase to products in a continuous delivery environment). At scale, the journeys are in production and are experienced by a large number of users. The data gathered about usage and environment helps enrich profiles and enables cognitive analysis (machine learning), which refines the interaction and further improves the experience.

As many journeys are digitized, they become interconnected, which leads to spontaneous discovery of new opportunities that have the potential for more emotionally engaging journeys. The beauty of this is that digital products can be added into the mix as this process continues. Once products go live in a commercial environment, the products embark on a maturity path or stage, which is called **evolve**. In this stage, the products enter a subsequent ideation phase, which again influences the formulation and enrichment of the journey. All along the way, a variety of data is being collected (acting personas, profile patterns, usage patterns) and tracked in a way that helps managers observe progress, assess problems, and understand new possibilities.

There are also underlying business benefits realized during this process. One is the relationship between the level of innovation and return on investment over time. The four stages of the cycle (or wave) each have a different economic impact (see diagram below). The goal for the business is to maximize return while evolving. The pod methodology, with its dynamic ecosystem, allows for economies of scale. As a company's journey progresses within these different waves, the cost per story point (see Glossary) decreases, paving the way for a second wave of innovation, all while maintaining capital efficiencies.

WAVES OF INNOVATION AND RELATED RETURNS IN THE NEVER-ENDING DIGITAL JOURNEY:

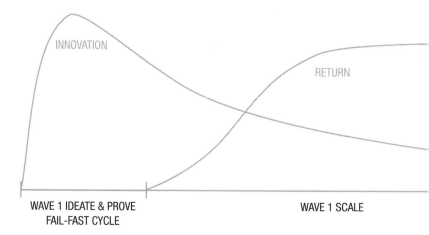

WAVE 1 IDEATE & PROVE
FAIL-FAST CYCLE

WAVE 1 SCALE

- *A more mature pod ecosystem delivers incremental returns due to improved journeys, more cohesive products, and better user engagement.*
- *Economies of scale are possible as more pods (development, evolution, devops) populate the ecosystem.*

A manager is able to view this entire process as if they were looking into a microscope, observing living cells growing and dividing before their eyes. The software tools help demarcate the relationships between pods at the ecosystem level as well as the various component dependencies, which are assigned different colors and notations. This macro view of the interdependencies and interactions also exposes what is termed a "critical path," which reinforces the correct and most efficient route for development in order to hit the market as fast as possible. Leveraging tools like GoPods (see Afterword) allows a company using pods to monitor the growth and any bottlenecks impacting the entire ecosystem. This allows managers to quickly and efficiently zero in on problem areas and address issues as they happen to correct course and continue moving forward in the realization of the journey.

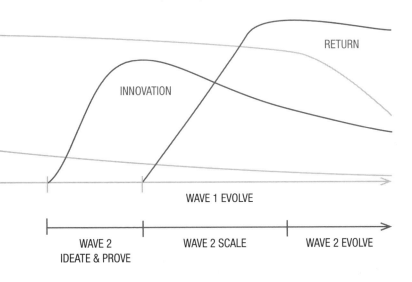

CHAPTER 5
SEEDING AND SCALING PODS

CHAPTER 5
Seeding and Scaling Pods

"THE CREATION OF A THOUSAND FORESTS is in one acorn," said the early American essayist Ralph Waldo Emerson. Emerson's elegant idea captures the intrinsic relationship between the seed and the unimaginable forest. This principle also translates to human endeavors, where the goal is to establish a sustainable environment in which an individual or organism can grow and prosper.

A pod, like an acorn, thrives in a supportive ecosystem with all the basic building blocks, such as people (biomass), diversity of talent (DNA), and competition. Similarly, the health of pods, like ecosystems, can be assessed by checking on specific indicators, such as mix of talent (nutrient cycling), production (energy regulation), and maturity.

As discussed earlier, pods and their very cross-disciplinary constitution of robust design, engineering, and innovation talents supply the growth factors to establish a balanced, sustainable, and replicable unit. Let's think of a group of pods as a means by which you can drive software innovation in a balanced way, much like the dynamics of a biological ecosystem.

In any living ecology, there is a balanced population of organisms; similarly, pods comprise an ideal number of eight people, each of whom has different and complementary functions—a blend of creative and engineering talent. Together, the pods have a kind of DNA that can be transported to another pod to help grow its functionality and capabilities.

Like biological organisms, the pods differ from each other in form and function. There are several different types of pods, each with characteristics that contribute to the overall process of software development (see Afterword).

MITOSIS

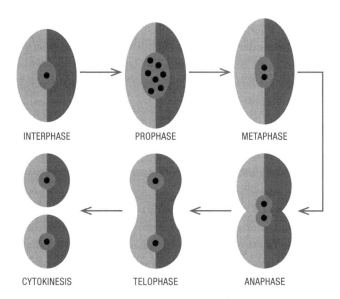

Pods grow, replicate, and propagate domain knowledge and talent in much the same way a living cell divides and grows into tissues and organs.

Just as in an ecosystem, pods can compete with one another. But unlike its natural counterpart, the outcome of that competition is not either surviving or dying. Rather, winning is an overall shared goal that helps interconnect pods. In other words, there are always incentives for pods to continue to mature and impact projects they are directly or tangentially involved in.

As pods grow and mature, working relationships between members are reinforced, and the collaboration also ripples through the business. It has a social impact throughout the company: when others see goals being met in a spirit of collaboration and fun, they're motivated to meet their own goals. In this way, the pod dynamics become an infectious agent, much like a virus, that can spread to other groups and motivate them. A pod ecosystem helps shape the overall experience and culture in an organization, which echoes Marshall McLuhan's insights about media and expression: "We become what we behold. We shape our tools and then our tools shape us."

As a pod matures, it generates its own DNA, which can then be used as starter material to generate a new pod. A piece of the pod, much like a cell dividing its nucleus, can be cleaved away and put to work elsewhere to help the pod grow and succeed.

For example, a few years ago a pod was created to help a large retailer explore new ways to manage its warehouse logistics and packaging schemes. The goal of the pod was to leverage expertise in big data, analytics, user experience, and mobility to maximize packaging efficiency. The ecosystem consisted of a Solutions Pod focused on the discovery process of the problem. It went into great detail and started creating the first prototype for the solution, destined to evolve over time. Over the course of the project, the data scientist of that pod was tasked with leading its efforts and eventually became its core member. Once the project was completed, that same data scientist could export his expertise and experience to generate a new pod tasked with a similar kind of software development project. The newly formed pod would gain greater advantage from the start by inheriting the core member's skills and capabilities as opposed to starting from scratch. This is how the pod model spreads its innovation DNA to other projects.

Pods help organizations and companies by establishing richer integration of design with engineering functions, along with several other secondary benefits outlined below.

EFFICIENCY THROUGH SIMULTANEITY

Agile pods help address the shortcomings and problems that software development teams face when collaborating on small- and large-scale projects. Companies face huge challenges in their software development processes due to wait times between teams, where one is waiting on another for a piece of code, or an asset, in order to move forward. This often leads to budget overruns and frustration. Within an integrated pod ecosystem, pods can work on various aspects of the project simultaneously, where the hierarchy of sequential events is fluid to prevent contention.

AGILE PODS: PROFILES AS ECOSYSTEM COMPONENTS

SOLUTION PODS

Roles: *Design, project management, development roles*

Activities: *Ideation workshops, brainstorming sessions, focus groups and demos, presentation to producers and executives, vision movie clips, prototypes*

Deliverables: *Omnichannel road maps, user journey, concepts, prototypes, cinematic visualization of the experience*

DEVELOPMENT PODS

Roles: *Development, design, embedded QA*

Activities: *Architecture and software development*

Deliverables: *Features and digital products, art assets, journey, backend components*

EVOLUTION PODS

Roles: *Development, QA, BA (if new feature is in scope) and design (new assets)*

Activities: *Scrum or on-demand feature delivery, ticket-based fixes, tech and biz analytics, user insight toolset*

Deliverables: *New features, fixes, user interface improvements*

DevOps Pods

Roles: *System, security, development*

Activities: *Fast-paced issue resolution, production operations, orchestration, hypercare, new features*

Deliverables: *Release management, infrastructure operations, KPI analysis, customer insight collection, reporting*

BETTER COORDINATION

As mentioned before, the pod ecosystem is continuously improving the efficiency of dependencies among pods. It allows companies to build prototypes fast and then iterate those designs to create viable new products. The pod becomes the glue that helps teams accomplish this protean goal, all while ensuring that design and engineering facets are linked together from the outset. In simple terms, think of art being applied to the company's content and science being applied to project execution.

STRONG BUT FLEXIBLE STRUCTURE

Pods help companies create a structure by which to coordinate the disparate parts of this dynamic building process. The talent within each pod morphs to adapt to the requirements— people leave pods, and new people come in. As long as the core members of pods stay motivated, pods can continue to scale, and add more velocity "muscle" when time to market demands. The ability to flex up and down capacity in both size and quality (seniority of members) allows the model to adapt rapidly to environmental changes, including changes of technology, trends, and budgetary constraints, among others.

BETTER PRODUCTIVITY MONITORING

Productivity metrics are at the center of the pods model, as they not only assess the relative contribution of pods to their ecosystem, but also anticipate when reshuffles of the ecosystem are necessary to adapt or correct deviations from business goals. They allow companies to monitor and create incentives that retain talent, which otherwise can be flighty. Talented designers and engineers aren't loyal unless they're engaged. Companies use the pod toolset to track their teams and identify problems and additional resources needed, thus giving the company greater insight into the operation and health of the software development project. And this toolset gives organizations better control over the outcomes and costs of development project work, as it can identify problems developing before they completely undermine the overall project.

REAL-TIME CRITICAL PATH AT SCALE

At the ecosystem level, the pods are related by order of dependency, i.e., which assets or software components they owe each other. Leveraging tools like GoPods (see Afterword), the critical path is calculated in real time, based on actual velocities and quality statistics as each pod has demonstrated throughout the course of the product road map life cycle. Thus, the accuracy of estimates is refined progressively. At scale, this creates enormous benefits to assess program status. This extreme visibility allows pod rebalancing—changing size and composition of pods, modifying scope feature priorities to make sure that actual product value is delivered as fast and cost-efficiently as possible. Every single product, project, and pod involved is subject to disciplined schedule, budget, and quality metrics, which accompany the typical pod metrics of velocity, quality, innovation, and autonomy.

CONTINUOUS IMPROVEMENT THROUGH MATURITY

Since their creation, pods are subject to a maturity path measured by a body of metrics that align to end product or business goals in time to market, quality, and level of autonomy and innovation.

GLOBAL PODS

The Internet and low-cost communications technology have drastically reduced the expense and difficulty of coordinating the work of global teams in faraway locations, while offering world-class technology assets and skills. Pods are not only scalable for large enterprise operations, but can also be leveraged across global time zones to deliver continuous twenty-four-by-seven software development.

In the past, this global work-flow concept of "follow the sun," whereby tasks are passed around daily between work sites on separate parts of the globe, has never been fully realized due to huge challenges, including high degrees of complexity in software handoffs, loss of managerial control, quality issues, communication gaps, security, and low morale.

But with their inherent focus on innovation, balance, and cross-functional capabilities, pods can serve as a repository in which software development efforts can be packaged and managed without the typical disruption caused by teams in one time zone not having enough context and communication to interpret code nuances and progress with the overall development. The benefits are significant in terms of reduced time to market and cost.

As pods help drive projects forward, all of the components and benefits outlined above help enrich the project as it evolves, leveraging the designer's influence and ideas. The pod is treated as a whole, not as the sum of its parts, and the whole has goals that are fully measurable.

Because the pod is designed as an inherently balanced entity (design, engineering, testing), it is able to evolve in the same way that a living organism can survive and thrive despite being faced with adversity and challenges. This is precisely how pods evolve and help supply companies with what they need most today.

In his 1978 award-winning book, *Lives of a Cell*, Lewis Thomas writes, "We live in a dancing matrix of viruses; they dart, rather like bees, from organism to organism, from plant to organism, from plant to insect to mammal to me and back again, and into the sea, tugging along pieces of this genome, strings of genes from that, transplanting grafts of DNA, passing around heredity as though at a great party."

Thomas's allusion to a "dancing matrix of viruses" and how they dart like bees is a powerful image through which to imagine pods and their infectious nature to other pods, and even to entire companies or organizations, as they function, thrive, succeed, and pass along useful traits.

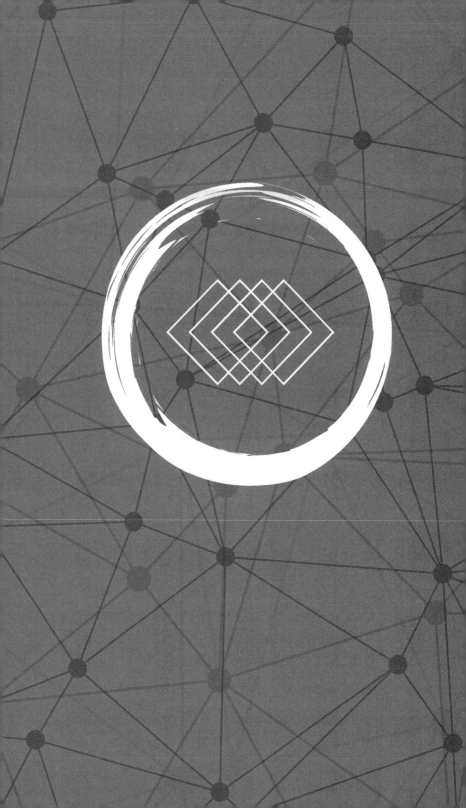

CHAPTER 6
THE POWER OF METRICS

CHAPTER 6
The Power of Metrics

A CROSS THE GLOBE, countries and firms compete fiercely to buy and sell products and services. At the heart of that drive is innovation, which is the cornerstone for sustained economic growth and prosperity. Innovation is a top priority for all shapes and sizes of companies, as well as countries. It's also powerful in catalyzing and transforming markets. When innovation is absent, companies and countries lag.

But maintaining potent innovation ecosystems and cultures that thrive and produce consistent output is extremely challenging. The nature of innovation is complicated, dynamic, and unpredictable. Innovation is such an elusive concept that even the definition of the word elicits a wide range of interpretations from business executives and managers. So it stands to reason that it has assumed mythic proportions across the business world.

The legendary twentieth-century economist Joseph Schumpeter said, "Carrying out innovations is the only function that is fundamental in history." His definition of innovation recognizes its opportunity for profitable change by driving new ideas into adoption and practice. Steve Jobs put it in simpler terms, "Innovation distinguishes between a leader and a follower."

"Innovation is a broad concept. It's not just about creating new products or services, but about change," writes Philippe Siberzahn and Walter Van Dyck in their book, *The Balancing Act of Innovation*.

Innovation is the cornerstone of sustained economic growth and prosperity. While innovation is often framed solely around breakthrough inventions, it can also be linked to changes across organizations as well as technology diffusion.

When it comes to the world of software, harnessing innovation translates into leadership. It gives companies a competitive advantage in today's all-digital markets. But the challenge is how to foster, measure, track, and sustain innovation in a balanced business ecosystem. At the end of the day, it's important to have a set of objective metrics, rather than relying on less than accurate subjective assessments. The trouble is, most innovation metrics are pretty loose and are more subjective than quantitative.

Measuring innovation at its most basic definition means determining how much is taking place and the value it's producing. Often the metrics used by companies to evaluate innovation can be misleading. These metrics might include something like the number of new ideas in various stages of development and the number of successful prototypes or products launched, all of which may improve the core metrics that define a business's performance. These measurements can lead to overestimation of the actual innovation that is taking place inside a company. Revenue derived from innovation is another problematic metric because it typically doesn't pick up the indirect business value improvements that certain ideas generate.

One of the challenges in maintaining objective metrics is that software development and innovation are largely practiced as a craft, not as a science. Most software development teams use qualitative assessments about the rate and output of their product, instead of objective measurements involving velocity, design iterations and quality, team members' productivity, user adoption, retention, monetization of products, features, new experiences, and cost per unit of product, among other aspects of the work. They are also so involved in day-to-day coordination, management of details, and turf disputes with other team members that they can lose sight of the process and goals of innovation, especially when the "innovators" are in one corner of the company or are inherited through an acquisition.

The pod model enables concise measurement, which allows pod members and managers to understand and adjust, if necessary, elements in the pods that can help boost the capabilities of the pod ecosystem.

All metrics combine to measure the level of maturity of the pod. Pod maturity is dynamic; it is not a status reached, but rather a flow of data that qualifies a pod at a given maturity level. **In its simplest form, the maturity of a pod is a function of its velocity, quality, and autonomy. These metrics help align three key requirements: translate business quantitative goals into software and experience metrics; incentivize vendors and**

consulting partners with rate increases each time the pods attains a higher maturity level; and reward pod members when pods mature.

Maturity levels are assigned through a grading process, which takes place monthly or quarterly, depending on the length of projects and ability to collect data points.

The very first step to baseline metrics among pods is to define a maturity criteria. The maturity criteria aligns metrics with the vision and connects the people within the pod (and among pods) with that vision.

The maturity criteria may be composed of two sets of metrics:

PRODUCTION METRICS specifically relate to the software development life cycle. We organized these metrics into four categories: Quality, Velocity, Autonomy, and Cost.

BUSINESS METRICS measure the impact of a digital feature, product, or journey in the business.

PRODUCTION METRICS

QUALITY
- *Experience value (focus group data)*
- *Code quality*
- *% of Green Builds (continuous integration)*
- *Code reviews*
- *Testing efficiency*
- *Bugs by severity by environment*
- *Sonar stats*

VELOCITY

- *Success record (velocity and unplanned work metric)*
- *Accuracy of estimations*
- *Stability of velocity*
- *Features release accuracy*
- *Productivity*

COST

- *Cost per story point*
- *Budget accuracy*

AUTONOMY

- *Core member ratio*
- *Seniority ratio**
- *Pod template compliance (missing roles)***

Objective metrics give managers clear, unfettered insights into what's working or not. These data points feed the pod maturity criteria formula to help determine the specific level of pod maturity of each pod, which in turn defines the maturity of the pod ecosystem.

*The seniority ratio is the percentage of experienced pod members who are considered "senior" (see Glossary).

**A pod template defines the composition of a pod in terms of roles and specific experience (see Glossary).

The **Production Metrics** table shows alternative metrics that could be selected to build a maturity criteria, which are broken into four fundamental categories: Quality, Velocity, Autonomy, and Cost. The following paragraphs explain the more representative metrics in greater detail.

QUALITY: Its data points are extremely valuable because they reveal how a feature, a product, or a digital journey is getting closer to expected functionality and behavior and how it is aligned with the overall vision of the experience.

The **experience value** metric uses focus groups to collect behavioral insights to determine how much value or how useful the digital product is to target users. These data points serve as input for new design-build iterations. The product managers and designers organize focus groups and launch beta versions to groups of users in a cluster group to obtain feedback. They contrast these findings with expected sentiment charts and user interface behaviors, which were defined when journeys were conceived and revised throughout iterative cycles. These practices help contrast actual data against the expected level of adoption, feature performance, and emotional engagement given by the digital journeys. The product owners engage a variety of professionals to analyze the data. In many cases, psychologist, sociologists, and domain experts review the results and provide structured feedback to product owners to guide them in refining features, channels, digital products, and journeys. These insights and design considerations are constantly fed into the pods developing the digital journey and building the required products.

As a companion to experience, which helps assess multiple dimensions of the user experience, it's important to measure the **quality of the code**. This can be performed through peer reviews or by using automation tools like Sonar, which check the code automatically during continuous building (when software is compiled and automatically tested) to detect bug patterns or suboptimal algorithms that may negatively impact performance (by either generating errors or impacting the sustainability and evolution of the software code). Peer reviews are useful as they add a human approach to the code review, which generally results in a more comprehensive code revision because it's done in pairs. Both automatic and manual code checks are complementary, and they should both exist in order to guarantee good quality.

An important metric in this process is the **quality of builds (% Green Builds)**, a measurement that captures the number of times a software build occurs and successfully passed automation tests based on many user case scenarios. The metric is generated from the ratio of successful number of builds over the total number of builds run. A build that fails frequently is very informative. It means either the code is bad and needs to be refactored or that it has many bugs that have not been fixed. Or it could reveal another important issue: the developers and automation testers are out of sync.

A build that runs every few minutes and is represented as mostly green (>95%) has much more likelihood of being at a higher quality (given by less bugs, highly covered by automated tests). Because this metric is fully automated, it is possible to read trends in real time. This benefits not only the individual pod but also all pods interconnected in the pod ecosystem. The real-time benefit allows managers to resolve problems immediately and reduces risk, well in advance of major milestones.

VELOCITY: This metric directly relates to time to market, which is a key category for production metrics. The metrics of velocity derive from data, which are calculated continuously during the course of a project. In physics, velocity is defined as the speed of something in a given direction. In software development, velocity is the rate of change of a product over time, which is why it's necessary to measure that digital component and figure it into the overall calculation of the velocity of the pod. There is plenty of literature about the many ways to measure these types of abstractions commonly found in software. To simplify, Globant uses "points" and assigns them to represent an equal "chunk" of product. Product features are broken into smaller chunks called stories, and each receives an assigned point estimate. For example, a ten-point story is "larger" than six-point story.

The **story-point unit** of measurement describes a user scenario that involves some kind of interaction between some form of software and a user, or another system. In simple terms, story points are the fundamental metric when it comes to calculating the pod or pod's ecosystem velocity. Because the metric tells how many story points are being completed over time, managers have great insight as to whether they're on time, ahead, or behind.

Sizing product features in story points helps a pod estimate product size, complexity, and its derivatives, such as velocity and cost. Each story is a kind of stepping stone, which, when combined, outlines a plan for the entire digital journey. For example, a story could be a person logging into Facebook, while another story could be the user then sharing some photo or comment across their social network. There might be, for example, 500 stories estimated in a project. With the number of story points and the expectation for having the prototypes done in a certain number of weeks or months, story points help determine if the pod is either ahead or behind in the planned schedule. If the pod is completing 50 story points per week, and the product is expected to be completed in five weeks, then there's clearly a disconnect. Either the estimates are too conservative (i.e., the 500 number is too high) or the completion expectation in five weeks is unrealistic because the pod is only able to perform at half the velocity required to finish on time. In this situation, the pod has to complete 100 points per week to deliver the project on time, though it's been proven that the pod has only been delivering 50 points per week. The power of story points is in their ability to refine   the scope of work and help alert and prompt discussions among pod leads, core members, and other pods in the ecosystem when inconsistencies or performance issues are encountered. Together the pods will use these data points to reprioritize and rebalance the pods' ecosystem so they can ultimately assess and make sure that velocity and quality meet the schedule and cost expectations.

In order to estimate how many points a story warrants, it's relevant to note that size in software does not linearly correlate to how many lines of code were written; rather, it is related to the number of back-end components to enable a story, the integration points with existing software that that story depends on, and the complexity of the logic and the user interface involved. Estimating story points can be greatly simplified by establishing guidelines that all pods follow.

As explained above, understanding the velocity of each pod allows a manager to determine whether features or products they are building will meet the expected deadline. What's more, it also allows managers and teams to calculate the velocity of a pod and the pod ecosystem and thereby assess with acceptable accuracy whether the entire development of the digital journeys is on track.

Another important point to understand about velocity is that it's fluid and directly influences the critical path of the digital journeys in real time. Examining the pod ecosystem exposes dependencies among pods, enabling managers to see which pods are creating bottlenecks within the software development life cycle. Identifying those problems creates opportunities for corrective action where there's contention, thus enabling an optimal flow that improves the overall time to market of a digital journey.

AUTONOMY: A well-functioning pod with a high potential to mature requires specific configurations and treatments. First, the pod needs to have a number of core members that have expertise in the business they are building a digital component for, beyond the design and technical chops required to the job. In many cases, there is a great deal of churn and attrition when it comes to industry or business knowledge skills, which can impact pods.

In order to create successful digital journeys, core members must have specific experience on how the business operates. Reaching core member status is a process, which needs to be defined and tracked. Tenure is an essential determinant of core status, as is the capacity of that person to produce incremental improvements, setting up a "working environment," where he or she can create guidelines and provide detailed examples that other members of the pod (a.k.a. extended members) can follow and expand upon. The metric that reflects this quality is "**Core Member Ratio,**" which is defined as the number of core pod members divided by the total number of people in a pod. Core member ratio is the best indicator of the level of autonomy of a pod. A higher core member ratio will typically lead to higher autonomy because the pod itself can translate high-level business rules or opportunities into executable stories and actual software without much help from anybody else. In doing so, the pod becomes a self-sufficient unit of design and execution.

COST: This category is related to other metrics and fundamental to determining the actual budget burn rate, contrasting that to how much is being produced. This allows a manager to understand how much good has been accomplished for each dollar spent. The most significant metric in the cost category is the **cost per point** (which can also be analyzed as an evolution curve over time).

The cost metric also demystifies assessing the worth of talent a company is hiring from vendors. In the traditional world of IT, vendors have won contracts based on their ability to scale particular talent and the competitive rates for such talent. This "cheap rate" approach has also been embraced by internal IT corporate projects to win corporate budgets, as it sells management the false illusion that more can be achieved at a lower cost. The pursuit of perceived lower talent costs has often led to myopic management decisions, which has negatively affected software development projects for decades.

In the era of digital journeys, the mind-set about cost is evolving. Businesses are no longer interested in hourly project cost metrics, but rather prefer the cost of output (result) and the ability to compare on a qualitative basis. For example, a pod could cost $50,000/month and finish a set of features with the expected quality in one month. By comparison, a pod that costs $25,000/month, but takes three months to finalize the same set of features at the same level of quality is more expensive. Let's suppose now the set of features in that project was estimated at 1,000 points. The cost per point of each alternative pod would have been: $5,000 for the first pod and $7,500 for the second pod. The superficially cheaper pod (given cheaper talent) is actually 50 percent more expensive as it takes more iterations to achieve similar quality.

This concept of cost per unit of product delivered is particularly important when it comes to working with partners or vendors that supply the talent to develop digital products. In these scenarios, it's important to analyze the relationship between velocity, cost, and the form of engagement (contract) between the parties.

Any business will benefit from understanding the cost per point, velocity, autonomy, and quality of each team (pod) of vendors. This approach realizes the actual value of a vendor as it relates to the digital journey that they are helping to design and build. This approach sharply contrasts with traditional fixed-price engagements in which padded estimates are used to cover vendors for risks. What's more, these fixed-price engagements lead to other problems, including change management processes. The pods structure and function embrace agility through a more sophisticated engagement where quality, autonomy, cost, and velocity become dynamic flows that can be managed in real time.

The diagram "The Pod Maturity Path Driving Efficiency" that follows shows the average velocity increases measured as reduction of hours to complete a story point. Level 0 depicts velocity metrics of teams working in similar technology and product that are not following the agile pod methodology. That is, Level 0 are staff augmentation contracts where the client sets all process rules constraining vendor independence and creativity; instead of "goaling" by results, they demand specific people with certain skills. The data was collected after two quarters, once Globant had enough samples at each maturity level. The amount of effort, in this case, takes into account total production time: time to define, develop, rework, and test within an iteration.

The metrics average data was collected over a six-month period. The levels in the X-axis of the chart are the maturity levels at which pods were performing along with their velocity. In this case, the number of hours to complete a point is measured (Y-axis). That is, fewer hours to complete a point means higher velocity.

THE POD MATURITY PATH DRIVING EFFICIENCY

AVERAGE PRODUCTIVITY (15 POD SAMPLE)

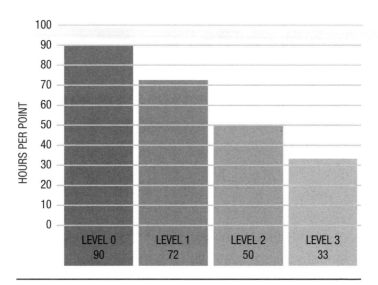

	LEVEL 0	LEVEL 1	LEVEL 2	LEVEL 3
	90	72	50	33

HOURS PER POINT

Now let's add the cost component to velocity. In this case, rate incentives were given to vendors whose pods performed at higher maturity levels. As we see here, seven pods promoted from Level 0 to Level 1 have achieved a velocity jump of 18 fewer hours to complete a point, when compared to Level 0. Even with an incentive of 10 percent to achieve Level 1, the pod is 12 percent cheaper, simply because it's much faster. Overall, with incentives, the pod ecosystem of 15 pods performs at 25 percent cost efficiency given the marginal gains in velocity being higher than the cost increase. The net results were: the marginal gains in velocity were significantly higher than the cost of the incentives.

HIGH MATURITY = HIGH PERFORMING TEAMS + HIGH COST EFFICIENCY

MATURITY LEVEL PROGRESSION	RATE INCENTIVE (Cost per hour)	VELOCITY GAINS (Hours per point)	NET COST IMPACT (Savings)	NUMBER OF PODS AT MATURITY
LEVEL 1	10%	18	12%	7
LEVEL 2	25%	40	31%	6
LEVEL 3	35%	57	51%	2
PROGRAM LEVEL COST-EFFICIENCY (Savings)			25%*	
TOTAL PODS IN THE ECOSYSTEM				15

*Weighted average

BUSINESS METRICS

Business metrics are another way to further align people, vendors, and the businesses participating in development of digital journeys. They can be part of the maturity criteria of pods or not. It depends on how the pod ecosystem has been configured, i.e., the number of in-house pods, the number of vendor pods, and the length and scale of the program.

Business metrics may not be applicable to maturity criteria for partners or vendors who are part of the pod ecosystem. Again, it comes down to context, or the specific nature of the partnership. In a traditional client-vendor relationship, there have to be clear incentives for vendors to put some skin in the game whereby they adhere to a maturity criteria in which business results are figured into the vendor compensation formula. Globant believes that evolved partnerships, in which there's an ongoing relationship among the parties, greatly benefit by business metrics being incorporated into pod maturity criteria. These metrics can be measured at the same time as production metrics and impact the level of maturity of the pod. An alternative form of alignment would be to define a percentage incentive or discount in vendor fees as a function of business metrics, outside of the maturity criteria formula. For example, a vendor would get a 10 percent bonus if business metrics were achieved after journeys have been in production for three months.

It's important to note that business metrics only make sense when they are designed in the context of a specific journey, within an industry. The limited number of examples below are here to illustrate some generic metrics, which need to be adapted to the particulars of each business.

MEASURING JOURNEY IMPACT

USER ACQUISITION: The number of new customers acquired through the feature, product, or journey being delivered

USER ADOPTION: The number of employees using a particular feature that makes a particular business work flow more efficient

RETENTION BOOST: The percentage increase of customers that remain loyal to a particular brand leveraging digital channels versus same number in previous periods

CONVERSION: The percentage of customers that purchase using digital changes, starting or completing a journey

SAVINGS BY AUTOMATION: The percentage of savings due to the digitization of defined set of processes

X-SELL: The percentage increase in purchase leveraging suggestion engine

UPSELL: The percentage increase in purchases leveraging suggestions to upgrade

ALIGNING GOALS THROUGH THE MATURITY CRITERIA

It is the powerful combination of production and business metrics that helps establish both short- and long-term alignment among pods, as well across divisions and partners involved in making the digital journey a reality. It is through the alignment of these metrics and their intrinsic goals that the maturity criteria emerge. Businesses realize specific gains from the synergy of applying and using metrics, and when combined define the specific requirements for maturity. As pods by their very nature and function comprise diverse roles and talents, the maturity criteria becomes the glue that helps ensure business and production goals work together despite political, departmental, or organizational boundaries that may exist.

MATURITY CRITERIA

METRICS	MEASURED	POD MATURITY		
		LEVEL 1	LEVEL 2	LEVEL 3
Velocity	*Daily*	*> 10 story points per week*	*Between 11 and 20 story points per week*	*More than 20 story points per week*
Product Quality	*Every sprint (iteration)*	*< 10 feature redesign identified*	*< 5*	*< 2*
Build Automation	*Daily*	*between 80% and 83% succeed*	*between 83% and 95% succeed*	*more than 95%*
Autonomy (Core Pod ratio)	*Monthly*	*10%*	*30%*	*50%*

Pods are motivated to improve continuously by raising their maturity level, directly benefiting the business by incentivizing partners and motivating employees.

MATURITY CRITERIA SAMPLE REWARDS

METRICS	MEASURED	POD MATURITY		
		LEVEL 1	LEVEL 2	LEVEL 3
In-House Pods incentive	Semi-annually upon maturity grading	Reward bonus +2 days off maturity star	2x reward bonus +4 days vacation 2 maturity stars	3x reward bonus +6 days vacation 3 maturity stars
Partner/ vendor incentive	Quarterly upon maturity grading	5% rate increase impacts next quarter services	10%	15%

The maturity level is a function of a pod meeting its metrics goals. The "grading" process (data is aggregated and compared with the goals) is performed either monthly or quarterly and assigns a maturity level to the pod, which often varies from zero to three.

The weight assigned to one metric versus others in the maturity criteria depends on the order of priorities for each business, such as experience, time to market, cost efficiency, etc. The maturity level will be awarded to pods as a function of the maturity criteria, which derives from this specific order of priorities. To illustrate, we describe below some hypothetical scenarios of weighing metrics priorities to determine the pod's maturity level in relation to its stage in the Digital Evolution Life Cycle (see Chapter 4).

A pod ecosystem in the ideation-prove loop (see "The Never-Ending Digital Journey" diagram in Chapter 4) may define a maturity criteria giving 40 percent weight to production metrics and 60 percent on business metrics, because prototypes at this stage are proven before they are scaled to become production-ready digital journeys. So, there's great emphasis on design and meeting the product quality goals, providing a better experience.

A pod ecosystem in the "scale" stage (see Chapter 4) may adopt a maturity criteria defined by a 60 percent weight on production metrics and a 40 percent weight on business metrics. At scale, time to market is critical to get to production quickly and at quality, in order to enable a phase of evolution that starts when users' insights are incorporated. A typical example is getting to a minimum viable product (MVP) successfully and iterating based on feedback, enhancing the product iteratively. In addition, production metrics may be more important at scale because there's likely a higher budget burn at this stage.

A pod ecosystem in the evolve stage, i.e., with a good number of journeys running in production, may have a maturity criteria giving 50 percent weight to business metrics and 50 percent to production metrics. In the "evolve" stage, it's critical for the digital journey to meet the business goals that will enable returns and activate another wave of invention. It's also important that pods perform and are cost efficient in order to fund the next wave of invention.

TRACKING POD STAGES

The pods management tool, or GoPods (see Afterword), integrates with several other development tools and pulls specific standard metrics to help it track and monitor these various metrics, such as productivity, quality, and velocity. By pulling in these metrics from development tools such as JIRA, Jenka, Sonar, Bamboo, and others, GoPods is able to automatically merge all this data around product quality and velocity and place the pod within a maturity path. In doing so, GoPods aggregate data to help update, track, and monitor the progress of the software development by pod, product, project, or the entire ecosystem. These various views will apply to different stakeholders; for example, a manager will be interested in understanding the schedule, cost, and quality of the product he is managing and will want to understand where productivity can compromise time to market, what component bottlenecks can affect delivery, what systematic quality issues risk launch, which products or features are not making the consumer impact required, etc. This data-collection mechanism, analysis, and dashboarding also works well in continuous delivery models where code is constantly being pushed into production in small chunks.

The more data the software development process outputs, the more integration and analysis capabilities exist, allowing GoPods to predict with high degree of certainty the overall product (or road map) outcome in terms of schedule, quality, and cost. What's more, it also allows leadership to adjust and rebalance pod ecosystems upon changes, reprioritization, user feedback, and new trends and technologies coming into play. This visibility enables faster reaction times to environmental changes, productivity issues, and talent deficiencies that are affecting the outcome of the product and impacting the overall digital journeys. Moreover, it creates a specific language, software development as science, that aims to minimize subjective assumptions and loose dependencies, replacing them with decision making fed by the pods velocity profiles, performance expectations due to their current maturity level, quality predictions based on current defect trends, automated build outputs, user's behavior towards software, and other concrete metrics.

These measurements help pods in two main areas. One, they allow the pod to redefine and adjust a process midstream. Second, they permit the pod to increase its velocity. Both of these measurements save a company time and money. With these tools in hand, a team manager can prioritize goals, assigning a weight to each particular goal involved in solving a business problem. This coordination becomes easier, with clearer communication and fewer disputes. And it allows a business to implement it in the ecosystem and generate results.

The bottom line is that good innovation outcomes are not only the result of a process or a model for valuing ideas, but of valid execution measurement, completed over functioning digital products. The stakes are very high in the all-digital economy, so without objective metrics integrated at every stage of the process, and aligned to top goals, a company risks its very ability to innovate and grow.

CHAPTER 7
IT'S IN THE GAME

CHAPTER 7
It's in the Game

I n April 2009, more than 15 million online video game players all over the world participated in a *Halo 3* game and celebrated a monumental milestone: 10 billion kills against a virtual enemy, the Covenant. *Halo 3* players spent 565 days fighting the third and final campaign in the fictional Great War, protecting Earth from an alliance of malevolent aliens seeking to destroy the human race. The online game marshaled the largest army on Earth as players came together. Once *Halo* players achieved this goal, there were virtual high fives exchanged between online players in forums around the world, both to congratulate one another and to claim their contributions. There was a widespread feeling of euphoria and accomplishment among the gamers.

Throughout the game, players shared tips and strategies and organized round-the-clock cooperative campaign shifts. In her book, *Reality Is Broken: Why Games Make Us Better and How They Can Change the World,* Jane McGonigal observes that this rich collaboration brought together a wide diversity of players and gave them a strong sense of purpose.

London *Telegraph* reporter Sam Leith likewise observed in his coverage of the *Halo 3* community, "What was once a solitary activity is now...overwhelmingly a communal one." The players were in it for each other and the rush of being part of something much bigger.

Gaming has become a central part of youth experience across American, European, and Asian cultures. The growth of gaming interest and influence is advancing at a rapid pace. According to Entertainment Software Association, 59 percent of Americans play video games. Smartphone device use has increased by more than 20 percent per year, and of those users, about 44 percent play games on them. In the United States, the average game player is thirty-one years old and has been playing video games for an average of fourteen years.

The result is that a high percentage of any workforce is made up of gamers—particularly among Millennials—and corporations are getting smart about using games as part of a business strategy, one that can achieve business goals while keeping workers interested. Gaming is no longer viewed as an individual pursuit, but a social one. Game proponents believe that games build stronger social bonds and lead to more active social networks. The more time we spend interacting with our social networks the more likely we are to generate a subset of positive emotions, which are referred to as "pro-social emotions." These are feel-good emotions— love, compassion, admiration, and devotion—that are directed toward others, and are considered crucial to our long-term happiness. They help create lasting social bonds that can be very helpful in motivating and maintaining a creative and efficient workforce.

For software developers, the massive interest in online gaming has revealed that gamers aren't just in it for themselves, but work together for social rewards. The fundamental recognition that players feel they are part of something bigger is at the very heart of pods. Gaming functions are built into pods so that software developers benefit from accelerating their collective goals—such as innovating around user journeys and experience, completing complex coding to bug-free software, and creating engaging experiences using multiple channels.

"Gamification" helps companies improve the overall productivity of developer teams. By creating a game environment, team members can collaborate and bridge divisions between creative and engineering teams and establish a richer, more flexible integration of a variety of technology skill sets. Pod members tap into the gamification mechanics by accepting challenges, customizable missions, and tasks that are molded into playful dynamics. From many customer experiences (see Case Studies), it is clear that gamification enriches collaboration, efficiency, and overall performance in software development projects.

While individual pods compete with one another in a game-like manner, the outcome of winning is a goal shared by all of the pods. It isn't about promoting one team member above others—

the overall accomplishments of the teams are celebrated, so that "game success" is ultimately the success of all pods.

At the heart of the game is an opportunity for players to focus their energy on something they see themselves as being good at (or getting better at) and enjoying. Psychologists and gaming experts say that the mental work involved in playing a game revs up one's cognitive facilities in what often can either be a rapid, condensed experience or one that is longer and sustained, as when players get involved in the simulated 10,000-year conquest campaigns in the real-time strategy game *Age of Empires*. As part of games, there's also discovery work that's undertaken by players where they actively investigate unfamiliar objects and spaces. That kind of work has been found to make people feel confident, powerful, and motivated.

In *The Innovators*, Walter Isaacson sums up the confluence of human interaction and technology giving birth to video games. "Video games helped propagate the idea that computers should interact with people in real time, have intuitive interfaces, and feature delightful graphic displays."

Brain researchers mapping the human brain have also embraced these powerful game concepts. In 2012, brain scientist and researcher Sebastian Seung started an online game called EyeWire that challenges the public to trace neuronal wiring (with computers) in the retina of a mouse's eye. It has attracted 165,000 players in 164 countries and was featured in a *New York Times* article. Seung and co-researchers created artificial intelligence algorithms for processing raw images. Players earn points as they mark, paint-by-numbers style, the branches of a neuron through a three-dimensional cube. Computers churn through the data, but the most powerful pattern-recognition technology known is the human brain.

The overall process of playing a game involves actively moving ourselves toward the "positive end of the emotional spectrum," writes McGonigal in her book, *Reality Is Broken*. "Games make us happy because they are hard work that we choose for ourselves, and it turns out that almost nothing makes us happier than good, hard work."

One benefit for companies is that the game model gives pod members strong incentives to stay in their current project, in the same way a person playing a game is motivated to advance to a new level. Pod members also get recognition by their pod peers as they help move the pod forward toward its common goals.

Tools like GoPods (see Afterword) provide pod members and managers with real-time reports of the progress they're making, which translates into a clearer view of their contributions and impact on the project. StarMeUp (see Afterword), another motivational tool, helps members reward their peers for jobs well done in multiple areas. All this helps award pod members "core member" status within pods, which allows them to move laterally across different pod projects, and eventually be promoted to become tech leaders and higher-level leaders within the pod ecosystem. A gamified career path makes progression fun, somewhat predictable, and minimizes the anxiety driven by interest friendships or political maneuvers to get higher in the organization. Smart, creative pod members seek meritocratic exposure, and many feel demotivated by organizational politics. Gamification helps expose the good members and drives people's careers based on pod results.

Pod metrics play a key role in tracking progress and goals, with rewards awaiting those individuals on the maturity path. Since pod metrics are collected continuously, it is possible to define rules and objectives that combine short-term goals and rewards on this maturity path. As pod members and teams achieve new levels in a game, so too do they advance in the hierarchy of pod maturity levels.

In addition to pod metrics, gamification design permits developers to align missions with overall product goals, such as productivity, velocity, and even certain aspects of the product and the intended market. These can include market-driven metrics like user acquisition, retention, return, or monetization. What's more, some of the micro goals within a maturity level give the pod credits, or energy. For example, an increase in velocity can award a pod an energy star, and that star can unlock prioritized access to a development environment, as well as perks for the pod members.

Pod members on the path to attain core pod member status do so by receiving a star from a peer, who helps credit that person to achieve their new status. As a core member of the pod, this designer or developer gains honor-roll status and receives an accomplishment bonus. With a wide range of incentive instruments, pod leaders can be as creative as they want when it comes to defining various incentives and rewards. The basic rule is that goals are clearly measurable and are applied consistently, with few or no exceptions. The objective is to avoid a complicated set of rules, incentives, and rewards, which typically creates confusion and proves to be counterproductive. That's why it's advisable to have a game designer define the mechanics, implement, and test results. GoPods (see Afterword) helps automate metrics collection and measure results upon implementation of gamification techniques.

Gamification is the carrot that retains talented workers who might otherwise defect to another company or startup. The important point is not to think about this as a transaction, but more like a seduction, just as one would encounter in the levels of a game. As a player gains more energy, he or she advances and the environment gets much richer. So it's not only monetary rewards being used to keep people engaged— it's better projects, training, a more strategic role, more responsibility or accountability, a different place to work with relocations, and many other alternatives that promote people's happiness at work.

The gamified style of career advancement empowers people to grow their skill sets and think longer term about where to go next. And it helps quench younger workers' drive to move to other companies because they've become bored. In the formulation of pod dynamics, the career path is very much part of the formula of maturity, which is aligned to the business goals. By rewarding people's investment of their time and career path, the pod model strengthens those overall business goals. It provides employees with the ability to move to other projects within the company, hence giving them more freedom to explore new facets. In doing so, these pod members have the added advantage of being able to plan their career in a more predictable way, which benefits both the individual and the company.

These principles and concepts are also relevant to making pods work for the Millennial generation of workers, who are between the ages of twenty and thirty. There are many cautionary tales warning of the woes of managing tech-savvy Millennials, and then there are those successful tech CEOs and founders who have blazed new paths and created new industries at places like Facebook and Tumblr by appealing to that group.

Managers have found that Millennials excel in a corporate culture where expectations are managed in an open and honest dialogue that emphasizes personal accountability and precisely defined outcomes. They like to know the "why" when it comes to making decisions. And they measure value by how many of their ideas a manager takes into consideration as part of the thought process. Pods help support and balance these issues for workers involved in software development projects.

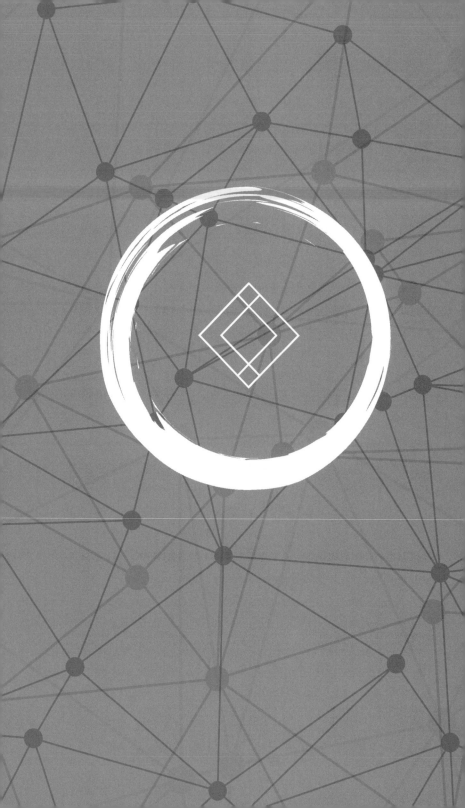

CHAPTER 8
ACHIEVING SOMETHING BIGGER

CHAPTER 8
Achieving Something Bigger

I N 1969, AT THE HEIGHT OF THE NASA Apollo moon program, a Tuesday morning news conference was held that has now become legendary. A newspaper reporter approached a janitor at the Kennedy Space Center and asked him about his job. He replied, "My job is to help put a man on the moon."

The story has come to symbolize the underlying importance of employees being connected to the overall purpose of their work, regardless of what they do. It is that core motivational alignment that helps drive innovation through rich collaboration across teams and organizations.

Innovation outcomes need to be tracked, measured, and fed with the DNA of maturity, so they have the necessary factors to grow, replicate, and scale (as outlined in the previous chapter). All of these are essential to the overall success of sustaining innovation, however, without the critical cultural elements, innovation is stifled.

What successful innovative companies have in common is a strong and resilient culture. But in order for the innovation culture to thrive, it has to be managed, refreshed, and refocused.

At Google, for example, the company culture and innovation can't be separated. As Google Chairman Eric Schmidt said in a Google document titled "Creating a Culture of Innovation," "You have to have the culture, and you need to get it right." It is all about having a diverse workforce, a multiform meeting-place of cultures, where people have different backgrounds, biases, and conceptual starting points in life and work.

Google outlines eight key principles necessary for creating a strong innovation culture. A few of those principles are: think 10x, which maintains that true innovation happens when you try to improve something by 10 times; launch, then keep listening, which emphasizes the importance of receiving real-world user feedback that helps to never stray too far from what the market wants; share everything you can, as collaboration is essential to innovation; and look for ideas everywhere.

These principles, when embraced with a strong level of commitment across a company, help create an environment where innovation is fostered, supported, and capable of taking on the same powerful dimensions like the DNA feeding it. Where companies run into trouble is when they sap the energy from a culture by trying to use reward systems that are counterproductive.

"For as long as we can remember, we've configured our organizations and constructed our lives around this bedrock assumption: The way to improve performance, increase productivity, and encourage excellence is to reward the good and punish the bad," wrote Daniel Pink in his book, *Drive:*

The Surprising Truth About What Motivates Us. But clearly, other metrics—such as engagement—are in play.

Pink lays out three elements that are necessary for motivation, all of which are integral to the pod methodology: autonomy (people want to have control over their work), mastery (people want to get better at what they do), and purpose (people want to be part of something that is bigger than they are).

Pink frames his thinking around autonomy by discussing great artists of the last century, such as Pablo Picasso, Georgia O'Keeffe, and Jackson Pollock. "No one told them, you must paint this sort of picture. You must begin painting at precisely 8:30 A.M. You must paint with the people we select to work with you. And you must paint this way," he says. Indeed, working outside those types of strictures, they were able to be much more productive and creative.

It's important to understand how maturity factors into the larger scheme of corporate governance, especially during this frenetic push toward the all-digital enterprise. As we have seen, companies are trying to grapple with the urgency of this big-stakes venture to embrace digital strategies and technologies to drive their brands and revenue.

As outlined earlier, many companies want to embrace digital technologies to help them get closer to their customers but don't have the technological means to get into the digital marketing space. Traditionally, CMOs come from a world of agencies, where they manage a brand with marketing strategies, campaigns, and initiatives. But when it comes to the technology skill sets, CMOs typically are unable to bridge the technology concepts into brand and vice versa.

The world of digital production is no longer project-based, but capacity-based. There is a shift from marketing campaigns to approach the marketplace, to developing capacities to reach channels across many platforms that involve following the journey of each user. Success is all about a company's capacity to create innovative digital journeys that customers interact with and deliver greater value to the company in terms of brand loyalty and revenues.

With pods, corporate executives can monitor and manage the process of innovating new digital technologies for the business in a much more predictable manner. In a pod ecosystem, a manager can use metrics to track how successful marketing, innovation, and delivery have been. All of which relates back to creating an environment that supports greater purpose, as outlined in Pink's book. That's basically how these pod ecosystems help transform a company into a digital technology enterprise. The ecosystem continues to be incentivized to deliver better results, while also helping to shape and grow the various talent pools that occupy these pods.

The reward-based system built into pods creates a driving force for team and individual members to meet and exceed their goals. These rewards aren't usually financial, but rather, team-building incentives, sharply in contrast to the "good and bad" reward system mentioned earlier. For instance, they might get travel or vacations, a mention in a newsletter, a push toward a role or a project they are interested in experiencing, a celebration at work, etc. Each pod has a name and identity, which helps establish common values and can leverage the client's brand image and create an environment where collaboration is prized. When individuals in pods reach the highest-level goals, they become a "core member" and can then move laterally to other pods with greater freedom within the company.

Rewards are administered like a role-playing game where experience points are awarded in a fun and dynamic way. This approach sharply contrasts traditional bonus schemes where this playful level of engagement is absent. What's more, the rewards experience is a socially shared activity that helps shape a distinctive personality for each pod. And it produces a stimulating effect that helps enrich, foster, and incentivize collaboration. As mentioned earlier in the book, the identity of the pod contributes to making a fundamental shift within the corporate culture: **evolving from assessing individuals to assessing groups with common goals**.

One of the ways executives can align their high-level business goals is by reviewing the pod maturity ratings of their teams. These ratings help identify strengths and weaknesses in the pods, which they can then adjust. The maturity level ratings help executives see performance from an objective level, which makes decision making easier and more effective.

Now let's expand beyond the confines of the organization. How does a product executive align vendors or partners to remain invested in the road map, make the pod model pervasive to their teams, and become engaged, not only methodologically but also culturally with the vision?

The executive can incentivize a vendor financially, and in turn, with those funds, the vendor can align its pods and make them part of the overall pod ecosystem. The maturity level of each pod is not fixed upon achievement, as it only lasts until the next assessment.

For individuals in the pods, these maturity goals can make work much more satisfying. It's a common situation for people to feel stuck at work as they search for validation in what they do. They want to know their contributions matter and that they are making a difference to the overall organization and its goals, which figures into how engaged they are to a project or company. Without maturity pods in place, employees are less likely to have a route to achieving some level of mastery in their job.

A Gallup research effort found that great managers possess five talents that align with motivation and purpose. First, managers motivate every single employee to take action and engage them with a compelling mission and vision. Second, they have the assertiveness to drive outcomes and the ability to overcome adversity and resistance. Third, they create a culture of clear accountability. Fourth, they build relationships that create trust, open dialogue, and full transparency. And fifth, they make decisions that are based on productivity, not politics.

In pods, one of the ways healthy competition is encouraged and managed is through gamification (see Chapter 7). As we've discussed previously, gamification adds an element of play to the collaborative project and goals. Just as a video game player would encounter different levels of a game to overcome, this dynamic can be used to drive more energy in the pod as it advances. In doing so, it is a kind of nonmonetary reward that keeps people engaged.

Part of the gamification involves competition between pods and relates back to creating ways for employees to get engaged into business goals and aspirations. "A friendly and healthy degree of rivalry will spur teams to think deeper and harder about a given problem, leading to new levels of creativity," wrote Bernard Ferrari and Jessica Goethals in their McKinsey report, "Using Rivalry to Spur Innovation."

Business analysts have found that employee engagement increases productivity and innovation, as well as stability, but until recently, companies haven't had a clear blueprint for how to create that kind of engagement. Pods give companies a structure in which employees can flourish, which in turn, enables the business to thrive. And it is pods' inherent organizational structural elements and roles that help reinforce how employees are connected to the overall purpose of their work, regardless of where they work in the business and what they do.

In large-scale enterprises or even small businesses, innovative companies have strong cultures where employees feel they're part of something bigger, just as the janitor for the Apollo moon program did. A culture has the power to stymie invention before it even has a chance to get started. But when a company is able to foster strong cultural principles and core values across organizational boundaries, the benefits blossom naturally, like a seedling nourished by soil, water, and sun.

CHAPTER 9
WHAT'S NEXT

CHAPTER 9
What's Next

S CIENCE-FICTION WRITERS AND NOVELISTS have been our modern-day prophets for envisioning the future, from Jules Verne describing ships being shot out of a cannon in his 1865 book *From Earth to Moon*, the seminal concept for space travel, to Arthur C. Clarke describing electronic papers much like iPads and tablets in his 1968 novel *2001: A Space Odyssey*. It is the power of our imagination that supplies the fuel to drive new insights and technological innovations and forge our digital journeys both as individuals and as businesses.

Our global digital economy is growing with extreme rapidity and diversity. Its growth has been derived from a rich combination of several software technologies, including mobile computing, social media, big data analytics, and cloud computing.

Mobility is no longer a buzzword. For most businesspeople, it's become a way of life that spans countries and crosses social and economic boundaries. We are all moving around with mobile devices that have shifted how we work, learn, and play. Software has become the glue by which every type of business and industry can boost its bottom line. In order to advance in this new era of rapidly changing digital software, projects should not fail once they have achieved full scale.

It's estimated that half of the gains in mobile Internet usage by 2025 will happen in developing economies, where an estimated three billion new users are expected to connect to the Internet, according to a McKinsey Global Institute 2013 report, "Disruptive technologies: Advances that will transform life, business, and the global economy." The drive toward hyper-connected devices and systems is expected to push great new advances, including autonomous cars, wireless power, 5G communication, and digital healthcare devices. We have music, games, movies, television shows, and access to digital library storehouses that make asking a question as simple as tapping or making gestures in front of all forms of user interfaces.

The more user-interface technologies advance, the more consumers and businesses expect. We want user-interface devices to do more and deliver ever more advanced, frictionless, and speedy interactions. In a few years' time, we'll look back at the digital world of today and consider it rudimentary, as we control all sorts of things, from our cars to our homes, via digital commands from mobile devices.

Mobility and big data have been a major theme in the evolution of human society over the past ten years. A few years from now, many of us will be immersed in an ultra-digital world, where virtually all aspects of our physical presence will be connected. Advanced mobile applications require ever-evolving, next-generation technology.

In this brave new world of unfettered access and fulfillment, companies can't afford to watch their competitors leave them digitally irrelevant to customers or to potential partners who expect these ideal user experiences. Having a strong way to digitally engage with customers is critical.

Looking into the future, hardware and software platforms will adapt to conform to the user's experience. What's more, the end user will be much less tolerant of the work-arounds they were forced to do in the past. As Millennials experience more than 50 percent of their lives through digital devices, the abundance of data allows for hyper-segmentation, beyond traditional socioeconomic segments, which helps create an inclusive category of diverse social and educational backgrounds. These new categories attract Millennials who may very well cohabitate the same marketing segment because they expect to live the same type of experiences.

The spread of the Internet and of digital technologies is transforming businesses and creating whole new ones. Global online traffic across borders grew eighteen-fold between 2005 and 2012, and could increase eightfold more by 2025, according to a 2014 McKinsey Global Institute report, "Global flows in a digital age." All of which is a prescription for software that creates less friction as users move from one platform or application to another in their journey. The experience is uninterrupted, as if you were moving from a café to a store and then onto an airplane. The number of interactions between physical points and the digital world through products and services is increasing exponentially. Technology traverses the life of consumers and employees under an invisibility cloak, solving common problems, suggesting good ideas, reducing overhead, and making things simple. Simpler journeys translate to exponentially higher reward for companies that can enable such experience, arrive faster, and challenge status quo with scale.

Digital technologies, which reduce the cost of production and distribution, are transforming flows in two ways: through the creation of purely digital goods and services, "digital wrappers" that enhance the value of physical flows, and digital platforms that facilitate cross-border production and exchange. The enormous potential impact of digitization is only beginning to emerge. Consider that international Skype-call minutes grew to 40 percent of the present level of traditional international calls in just a decade. Or that cross-border e-commerce has grown to represent more than 10 percent of trade in goods in less than a decade.

An environment of things that connect to a set of user experiences across devices, screen resolutions and sizes, and interface metaphors (from pushing buttons to making gestures) makes the developers' lives more complex, and also makes the ecosystems that develop these products more complex. What's more, companies need to embrace more sophisticated engagement strategies with partners that reflect and synergize with their own culture.

Organizations are using technology to connect with

consumers and establish a dialogue with them. For some companies, this is the first time they've established a digital dialogue with their customers. And the software to make this happen must be easy to use for both the company and the customer—so simple that in a matter of a few seconds a consumer can figure out how to communicate ideas and create some value from that interaction, which helps initiate or continue the digital journey. The importance of involving designers early in the process helps validate what should be in the software.

"The next phase of the Digital Revolution will bring even more new methods of marrying technology with the creative industries, such as media, fashion, music, entertainment, education, literature, and the arts," writes Walter Isaacson in *The Innovators*.

It's a challenge for existing industries and businesses to play catch-up with upstart digital tech companies, which tend to be much more agile and user-friendly, as in the case of a company like Uber for ride sharing. They began with a simple premise based on user experience: customers wanted to get a taxi to their door or business without making a phone call. The car shows up where you are and arrives as predicted, and the customer can track its progress, and doesn't need an additional interaction for payment. This kind of positive user experience builds momentum and a community around that "friction-free experience."

One of the earliest of these frictionless experiences was

Apple's pioneering method of downloading music with iTunes. It offered a way for a customer to buy a single song over the Internet instead of having to go to the store and buy the CD or album. Other digital tech startups followed this path, such as Pandora and Spotify, which offer consumers a way to listen to music by simply subscribing. All were experiences that the community wanted. But these innovations only came about after digital music companies had been engaged in a "conversation" with these customers to understand their wants and needs.

The push toward developing digital solutions at scale will require cultural changes across businesses and the IT organizations supporting them. And that won't come easy for many large firms, because the central thrust to make this happen revolves around the integration of design and engineering skills and capabilities.

Similarly, there are hurdles for companies trying to achieve this "all-digital journey," which requires a new organizational architecture in which emerging digital processes coexist with traditional ones. Some experts have suggested this coexistence requires creating a two-speed architecture: a fast speed for evolving customer experiences, and a transaction speed for the remaining functions, where the pace of adjustment can remain more measured, according to a McKinsey Quarterly article (December 2014), "Running your company at two speeds." But pulling off this split typically means confronting a framework of IT practices and organizational processes, which have evolved over time and are at the core technology infrastructure keeping businesses running. "Digitization has led to bifurcated competition that challenges monolithic corporate structures. A two-speed approach to architecture will help companies navigate what's likely to be a tricky period of transition," McKinsey authors wrote.

There are many companies making the shift to establish a continuous digital conversation with customers. One recent effort worth noting is Disney's, as described in an article in *Wired* magazine, "Disney's $1 Billion Bet on a Magical Wristband."

The article describes a major digital initiative of Disney's newest innovation, MagicBand, which allows visitors access to Disney World in Orlando, Florida, and replaces every transaction a visitor would make during their experience, ranging from rides to restaurants and gift shops. The MagicBands look like simple, stylish rubber wristbands offered in cheery shades of grey, blue, green, pink, yellow, orange, and red. Inside each is an RFID chip and a radio like those in a 2.4-GHz cordless phone, with battery power that will last for two years.

Visitors start to learn about how to use their MagicBands when they book their reservation. The preferences for a visiting family, for example, are packaged into an itinerary for the park. When the family visits the entertainment park, they may decide to pick a restaurant for lunch. A Disney World app lets the family order food in advance. The MagicBand allows the family to make a reservation and also conveys their name to the host who greets them. And it's linked to the customer's credit card, so the bill can be handled simply and swiftly without friction.

The MagicBand is embedded with a long-range radio that can transmit more than forty feet in every direction. Inside the restaurant, there are radio receivers on the ceiling that permit the application to triangulate and determine the location of any MagicBand. So when the family sits down, the host and servers know where to bring the meal they've ordered. The article asks the question related to this all-digital experience at Disney World wearing a MagicBand: "Will the world at large ever become something akin to Disney World, loaded with sensors attuned to our every move?"

And the answer is most certainly that the road ahead is paved with these kinds of enabling digital technologies that create a frictionless experience for the customer in all kinds of business environments.

As companies push into digital consumer markets, they encounter challenges around coordination, communication, and scaling their efforts. Rethinking processes and embracing new models by which to create and drive innovation requires focus and open-minded approaches. For companies looking to get on the digital fast track, trying to attract outside talent and build a culture around innovation and digital technologies is also very challenging. It is difficult to find those people who have the DNA that can create a compatible digital vision inside a traditional corporate environment. It is also critical that the transformation agent be empowered to make changes. The intersection between these requirements (the empowered visionary and a team that can actually execute from within the company) renders a few choices, seldom scalable to make innovation happen. Hence, companies are partnering up with pure digital native companies and creating pods.

The very nature of innovation is often misunderstood within company cultures. And there is a pervasive myth that great innovations were largely driven by the individual, like Thomas Edison inventing the light bulb, Alexander Graham Bell inventing the phone, and Eli Whitney inventing the cotton gin. Their ideas didn't spring forth in isolation like a volcanic eureka moment, but rather were created and driven by incremental improvement.

"Simultaneous invention and incremental improvement are the way innovation works, even for radical inventions," Mark A. Lemley writes in his paper "The Myth of the Sole Inventor." His paper focuses on the history and problems of patents, but also chronicles the history of the nineteenth and twentieth century's most famous inventors. For example, legend says that Samuel Morse was having dinner with friends and debating electromagnetism when he realized that if an electrical signal could travel instantly across a wire, why couldn't information do the same? Actually, the telegraph was invented by not only Morse, but also Charles Wheatstone, Sir William Fothergill Cooke, Edward Davy, and

Carl August von Steinhiel. They were so near to each other that the British Supreme Court refused to issue one patent, according to Lemley. What's more, it was Joseph Henry, not Morse, who discovered that coiling wire would strengthen electromagnetic induction. Morse's key contribution was the application of Henry's electromagnets to boost signal strength, which, Lemley says, "it is not even clear that he fully understood how that contribution worked."

Writer and historian Walter Isaacson sums up the same points in *The Innovators*. "First and foremost is that creativity is a collaborative process. Innovation comes from teams more often than from the light-bulb moments of lone geniuses," Isaacson writes.

When companies try to create their own in-house teams to tackle today's digital technologies, they run into several challenges surrounding management and how the overall process and people are structured. Established structures in traditional mind-set companies are harder to bend and make flexible. For example, think about the prospects of a new digital team that requires building new kinds of digital products. They begin by engaging their top IT architect. The first order of business for that architect is to procure a new software toolset. But the company's IT department doesn't have this vendor on its list of approved vendors. This can set the team back several weeks as it tries to figure out how to get around restrictions and constraints from IT and legal department requirements for compliance. This issue may be easy to fix, but what if the architect is tasked with creating consumer products that leverage the social sphere, which require adoption and engagement to drive brand equity or create additional revenue streams. Can a highly skilled technical person create a team that deals with all these dimensions? In most cases, technical teams led by engineering principles prefer to invent "solo": without continuous input from their target audience, they simplify how they work to increase productivity and they tend to insulate themselves.

Now, let's look at the same scenario from the opposite angle. Can a highly skilled designer or product lead create a team that not only solves for customer acquisition or engagement, but also integrates with existing business processes, technology stacks, and development methods?

We agree with Thomas Lockwood's quote from his book, *Design Thinking: Integrating Innovation, Customer Experience, and Brand Value*: "Culture and design are interdependent." The challenge of driving innovative, thoughtful design for digital applications requires effort and a certain kind of awareness. Integration is both tricky and crucial to success. In order to nurture and harvest software innovation as technological complexity increases, businesses need to have a means by which to keep the integrated ecosystem balanced and moving forward.

"The greatest design thinkers have always been drawn to the greatest challenges, whether delivering fresh water to Imperial Rome, vaulting the dome of the Florence Cathedral, running a rail line through the British Midlands, or designing the first laptop computer," Brown writes in *Change by Design*. "They have searched out the problems that allowed them to work at the edge because this was where they were most likely to achieve something that has not been done before."

The innovation riddle that companies have to grapple with is how to control costs and scale innovation efforts as markets demand new ideas and products. Shifting customer demands requires that companies are very agile in building their new software, testing as they go along.

When the digital product doesn't meet its consumer acquisition, engagement, retention, or conversion goals, the team is forced to iterate, only if the business has given them another chance. The business is generally the internal buyer of the solution in these environments, not the maker. All these acquired structural and behavioral patterns prevent the team from delivering the product at the right time, and though the market may be forgiving, in most cases, the opportunity window can be quickly closed by a competitor that launches its product first.

With large, established businesses, innovation efforts feel like you're trying to turn a very large supertanker. It takes a lot of energy, and sometimes it feels like the mission of innovation is doomed before it begins. But what if the supertanker was helped by several smaller boats in the water? They can be more nimble in their movements, but still can support the bigger ship and its overall mission.

Pods have an inherent nimbleness, largely from their constitution of skills and talents being cross-functional. With these assets, they can assemble and connect to the "mothership" by injection, i.e., using specialized talent from studios purely conceived to deliver new and innovative experiences, without previous agendas or political boundaries.

"The Scientific Revolution, the Enlightenment, and the Industrial Revolution all had their institutions for collaborative work and their networks for sharing ideas. But to an even greater extent, this has been true of the digital age," writes Walter Isaacson in *The Innovators*. "The innovation will come from people who are able to link beauty to engineering, humanity to technology, and poetry to processors."

In this new era, the bar for businesses has been raised considerably around digital technologies. In order to compete, and to have a rich digital conversation with consumers and employees, companies need to be nimble. The first step to that agility is having creative and engineering functions integrated, which helps to ensure a frictionless customer experience. Integration also allows for faster delivery, faster pivots, and cost efficiencies. In order to have sustainable innovation, companies have to nurture it, and pods allow for that kind of evolution. Kickstarted and supported by consistent top management alignment, once pods mature, they can become viral, forming an ecosystem that provides the cultural and methodological structure to contain, measure, and foster a never-ending digital journey. The journey of the consumer and employee, in a continuous experience improvement loop, is the same as the journey of the business, also incrementally adding value and increasing returns, listening better and adapting faster. Pods help build the next generation of digital talent savvy with the viral potential to evolve the DNA that helps companies to "reload" as digital natives.

EPILOGUE
THE NEW DIGITAL
DESIGN GUILD

EPILOGUE
The New Digital Design Guild

EVER SINCE ARTISTS STARTED using the term "studio" centuries ago, it has come to be associated with a person or group that possesses a zeal for study in both their work and what they produce. Historically, the artist's workroom has been a physical space, used for a variety of purposes—architecture, painting, pottery, sculpture, woodworking, animation, photography, music, film—but now it is being used as a virtual concept, one that can help companies grow. Leonardo da Vinci once said, "An artist's studio should be a small space, because small rooms discipline the mind and large ones distract it."

One can think of the role of the studio as part of a biological ecosystem. The innovation that comes from the studio plays a critical role in the pod's ecosystem and becomes the catalyst that delivers energy to the cell. From that infusion of energy, or innovation, the pods are enriched so they can better adapt and address the challenges facing them.

Studios are a good example of how talent can develop and thrive, but they are not sufficient to realize innovation when standalone. Pods combine talent. And the model makes it easier to combine such talent as it's designed to support the creation of pods.

Ultimately, studios help supply pods with the necessary building blocks to create new designs, craft road maps, and move forward. High-level expertise in any of these studio areas can be critical for an organization's success in innovation.

The idea that a disciplined software engineering process is central to information technology is evident across many successful customer engagements over the past decade. However, it must be combined with creativity and agility in order to drive innovative solutions that address business needs. One way to think about this is as if the left side of the brain meets the right, where it explodes with concepts and ideas that can actually be realizable. Some studios have a balance of technical and creative expertise, while others are purely creative. They work synergistically with the overall objective to have design and engineering capabilities working together in any pod and in any business.

Today's rich landscape of emerging technologies supplies companies with great opportunity for innovating and creating strong digital products. Among the spectrum of technologies are all kinds of intelligent sensors, beacons, and home appliances. And these become the sparks that catalyze new innovations for the marketplace. Housing focused practices involving these many emerging technologies are what studios are designed to do. A studio has three to five different practices. When the trend for a specific set of technologies shows more momentum and traction, these become opportunities for initiating a new studio devoted to the technology.

In essence, studios are focused R&D labs that create the capacity and capabilities that scale innovation. The studio staff plays with cutting-edge ideas and technologies, constantly pushing the envelope. These studios are able to accomplish, on a small scale, the innovation cultivation that is essential for a balanced and thriving innovation ecosystem—and critical in today's markets and across countries and geographies. The main difference to just trying out cool prototypes in a lab is that studios grow specialization systematically and at scale— specialization roles are defined, training plans are created, talent is recruited, and the result is a concert of parallel activities that are subject to projected demand and a measured dose of risk betting on certain technologies and trends— talents that are going to be required in the future.

The following chart depicts how Globant captures emerging trends and technology and develops studios, whose members combine as pods when they are designing and building digital journeys for clients.

GLOBANT LABS	GLOBANT STUDIO
Emerging tech or trend prototype is adopted by one of our 12 studios.	Studio matures tech and brand into a practice: standardizes processes, increases capacity and builds solutions.

AGILE PODS
Practices members from the Studios are combined into Agile Pods for project execution. Diverse Studios bring expertise, thought leadership, processes and solutions and specific industry acumen when executing projects for our customers. The goals of our client become parameters that determine "Pod Maturity".

The dynamic flow of emerging technologies is a viral progression from labs to studio to pods, where its maturity impacts everyday digital businesses.

Studios are able to deliver to companies all the elements of innovation that would be difficult, if not impossible, to address on their own. The U.S. government's National Innovation Initiative (NII) undertook a two-year study to better understand how to foster innovation. Among its 2012 findings, it found that innovation has become:

FASTER: Technology advances are diffusing at ever-increasing rates. It took fifty-five years for the automobile to spread to a quarter of the country, thirty-five years for the telephone, twenty-two years for the radio, sixteen years for the personal computer, thirteen years for the cellphone, and only seven years for the Internet.

MULTIDISCIPLINARY: The most valuable innovations often arise from the intersections of different fields or spheres of activity. Fields like bioinformatics or nanotechnology did not even exist a few decades ago. Today, many economists believe they will become major drivers of the future U.S. economy.

COLLABORATIVE: As innovations become more technologically complex, they require active cooperation and communication among scientists and engineers and between creators and users.

DEMOCRATIZED: Innovation used to be the domain of research and development departments. Today, more workers and even customers are involved in the innovation process. Firms in industries as diverse as software and food flavoring are providing tools to customers to design their own products.

GLOBAL: Innovation can originate anywhere. Increased education and economic growth have improved the capacity of developing countries to offer new products and services. Modern communications and transportation technologies allow these countries to share advances with consumers across the globe. As a result, great ideas—regardless of where they originate—are less likely to be lost in our increasingly interconnected world.

Studios deliver powerful benefits across all five of these innovation factors. It is an integrated approach that reinforces a highly differentiated value proposition summarized in these three core tenets: organization by technology-specialized studios; emphasis on a collaborative and open culture; and innovation and creativity in technology and design. A key part of this relentless drive is best summed up by Tim Brown in *Change by Design*. "We are at a critical point where rapid change is forcing us to look not just to new ways of solving problems but to new problems to solve."

The rapid pace of technology and innovation is challenging industry incumbents and paving the way for unimaginable advances. All five of the factors outlined above are deeply tied into the role studios play in this relentless drive to create innovations, all of which are informed and driven by design and art.

For more than a decade, we've worked closely with our customers across the globe and witnessed industries pivot and companies shift to adapt and ride the new digital wave. Over the course of these engagements, we have evolved, adapted, and built, piece by piece, the foundation for agile pod methodologies and studios to help our customers realize their boldest dreams. Our own digital journey reflects and embraces the many different journeys we've helped our customers craft and realize as they take on big challenges in our ever faster-moving global economy. Our mission is to continue the journey we embarked upon in 2003, which drives us to invent, realize, and help our clients build rich digital connections with their customers, tailored to delight and surprise in a powerful way.

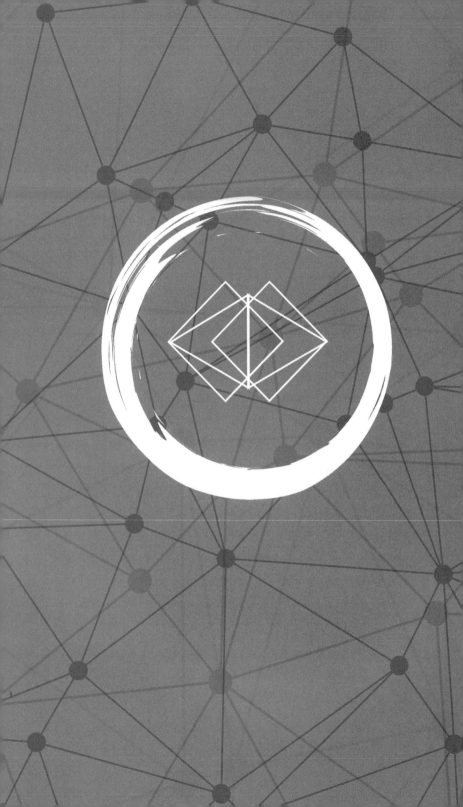

APPENDIX
CASE STUDIES

APPENDIX

Case Studies

A NOTE ON THE CASE STUDIES

S INCE ITS FOUNDING IN 2003, Globant has delivered thousands of projects, using its highly innovative software development pod methodology and services, to hundreds of mature businesses across a variety of different industries. The company has helped steer these projects for its clients and observed in the process a variety of practices and symptoms that thwart innovation, including divisions rooted in turf battles and collaboration that is mandated but not natural.

In order to illustrate its pod principles, Globant has outlined seven representative case studies culled from an internal company crowd-sourced effort that spanned 4,000 employees and many countries and geographies. The goal with these case studies is to help drive home key benefits derived from the pod methodology and practice so readers can glean their own insights and apply that perspective to their own projects. Client names and product names have been removed to protect privacy and confidentiality.

Each of the following projects or case studies has a

specific kind of personality, and while it operates with all of the fundamental properties and functions of a pod, the characteristics of the project emphasize one aspect of the six key elements of a pod: time to market, people, cost, experience, scale, and innovation.

These case studies will help readers understand how pods nurture and support software innovation in a balanced manner, much like a dynamic biological ecosystem. Striking a balance is critical when it comes to making a pod ecosystem function properly. And sometimes an imbalance can undermine the overall objectives.

Globant believes these real-world examples of projects will provide readers with concrete stories that speak for themselves in terms of illuminating the benefits derived from our work over more than twelve years. Along the way, our clients have changed as well, and we expect that there will certainly be more changes to come as we traverse new problems facing industries and companies in the digital realm of doing business.

NEW WORLD DIGITAL COMMERCE

W HEN A COMPANY is invited to participate in a project, it's always a very welcome recognition of good work. It's even more gratifying when the company inviting your participation is a behemoth in the world of digital commerce and technology.

Globant received such an invitation in October 2012 to help a leading digital company, "D," revamp its e-commerce platform. The proposal deadline was only two days away and the actual project time line was extremely ambitious, scheduling only several months for rebuilding the entire e-commerce platform. Most software development service companies would balk at these nearly impossible deadlines, or decline the invitation altogether. But Globant moved forward with the opportunity.

The next day a call was convened and the project goals, time frames, and outcomes were discussed. The first step was to confirm Globant wanted to participate in the project. Second, Globant would need to deal with the short deadline and project time frame. Globant asked for a few days' extension to allow time to submit a proposal. It was October, and D wanted to have its e-commerce platform ready in a few months—a fixed deadline that couldn't be budged. That left the team with only a few months to complete the complex and demanding project.

The other point of contention was the scope of the project. Globant's team made it clear that it wouldn't be able to fit everything mentioned in the Request for Proposal (RFP) within the time frame. That meant agreeing upon what the minimal viable product (MVP) would be for the project. Other elements were also discussed, including the specific kinds of technologies and specifications, project goals, and other details.

"We had little time to spare, so we immediately assembled a pod to work on the proposal," said Kevin Janzen, Globant client partner. "We knew the pod had to be an interdisciplinary team with a wide range of different skills and expertise."

For the e-commerce platform, those skill sets included load and performance balancing, interface design, front-end development, back-end development, and mobile experts. Globant also had technical architects, product managers, project managers, and interface and visual designers working together to define a technical approach and delivery plan.

The pod delivered its proposal by the end of the extended deadline. Its technical approach focused on scalable, quick-to-market, iterative development.

"We didn't want to reinvent the wheel, so we looked for an available framework that met most of the functional requirements and that leveraged the same technical stack that our client was used to," Janzen said. "We reached out to them and quickly got them on board with the process to ensure the estimations and assumptions were on the right track. D told us they were impressed about how spot on we were."

Globant's immediate concern became how to quickly staff the project. Assembling forty people with the right skill sets in one single location was not possible within the time limitations, which called for beginning the project within three to four weeks. After internal discussions, Globant realized its best option was to staff the project in four different locations. This distributed team approach was not a problem, as Globant had experience managing projects in diverse locations.

The first step was to divide the teams in a logical way, which was by functionality. In doing so, each team owned a portion of the overall project. This also meant that each team would need to establish strong leadership while working with multiple teams. Finally, the pod determined it would need a strong Globant representative on site with the client.

By the end of the fourth week, Globant had everything in place with only a few positions left to staff. They had a strong pipeline for candidates, which was helpful when the client decided to increase the scope of the overall project and add even more functionality to the e-commerce platform. That change didn't roil Globant, as its pod structure and process was already in place and working.

"As we approached the final phase of development, everything was right on track," Janzen said. "What's more, we were the only group of this large project that was within budget and delivering on time."

Looking back, the key to making the project work was the initial analysis the pod performed when it approached the project with a cautious sense of respect for the ambitious goals and scope.

D had talked to many vendors, but had dismissed every one of them that wasn't scared about the project. One of the deciding factors for D was that Globant recognized how challenging the project was from the outset. A key takeaway for the engagement was how the pod model helped the team efficiently focus and realize the project's fundamentals and goals concerning the unknowns, the critical path of dependencies, and then create an elaborate plan to solve all of these dimensions. What's more, the pod helped sort out the correct sequence of activities that established an environment of collaboration and risk mitigation before the first line of code was written or any asset was designed. Globant's attention to these elements was a key deciding factor for the company.

ONLINE GAMING

O NLINE GAMING GIANTS LIKE "H" create virtual environments in which players compete to win rewards. When online gamers compete, they like their virtual environments to simulate the physical world. Players purchase virtual items to help them win the game and defeat their opponents. It's become common for large gaming companies to deliver an integrated, seamless way by which these virtual goods can be purchased as players compete. But oftentimes, the devil is in the details in getting these commerce platforms to work in real time.

H's main goal was to create a micro-transaction system so that gamers could purchase virtual goods without slowing down the momentum of the game. Transactions were taking minutes when they should have been taking less than a second.

H had been wrestling with this challenge of connecting an e-commerce engine to its online games so the experience for customers was uninterrupted. They called in Globant to help create a fast solution. The challenge was stepping into this three-year-old project, which had little success to show for its efforts. The project had gone over budget, and H desperately wanted to find a solution so it could better monetize its entertainment efforts. The Globant team entered to help resolve the problems and implement a new solution that would catalyze H's e-commerce goals.

"We were the driving force for many changes, such as keeping the product up-to-date with technology trends," says Carolina Dolan, a client partner at Globant.

The pod took over the project and quickly found mismatches of technology and business needs. The team started suggesting changes, such as removing licensed software that was not being used, and evolved the solution into a development environment that was more flexible.

"When we joined the project, it had already gone over budget and was overly ambitious," Dolan said. "Our agile methodology and our focus on leveraging open-source solutions where appropriate allowed us to introduce a vision that had been lacking and reduced time to market."

All of these changes occurred while taking into account the overall release schedule for the project. But changes also came the other way around when Globant realized that H needed to change the business model of this particular product and in the short span of three weeks, the pod created a proof of concept.

An important milestone in the project was when two of Globant's team, over the course of the weekend, removed the existing commerce system that engineers had not been able to make work. "We told the employees that when they come back on Monday morning, there would be a new system in place for them," recalled Dolan. "We not only helped evolve the product, but allowed our teams and engineers to also grow with the products and find new career opportunities within the team. We had QA and system administrators who transitioned into being developers, and there were business analysts and developers who transitioned into project management."

"The company realized it needed to change the business model of this particular product and we went along for the ride, starting with a proof of concept. The project continued with the development of the new product while retiring the previous one over the following months, with a team of thirty or more people divided into three separate pod feature teams."

Dolan attributes the successful outcome to a few factors. First, Globant had enough empowerment from the client to become a driving force. Second, each of the pods was a self-organized unit with full knowledge of the platform, which meant there was a huge focus on quality as the three units worked cohesively to minimize the impact on cross-team dependencies. "This allowed us to not only evolve with the product, but also allowed our teams and engineers to grow with the products and find new career opportunities within the team," Dolan said.

What's more, it was run like a true partnership. Globant's initial project and involvement with H turned into a long engagement of five years.

21ST-CENTURY COMMERCE

WHEN A GLOBAL entertainment company, M, recognized its e-commerce platform was becoming obsolete and costly, it realized it needed a full overhaul of its infrastructure to meet the growing demands of its digital business online. The goal was to revamp the company's technology infrastructure from top to bottom to ensure it could better position itself for its business across international boundaries and cultures.

The existing legacy systems that handled its e-commerce business were expensive to maintain, so revamping the infrastructure with a new system looked good for long-term savings. M knew that it needed a strong technical team with skills the client did not have in-house to transform its aged systems into twenty-first-century digital infrastructure. Finding the people and scaling the effort would be big challenges, as the project team was spread from California to Florida to Europe and China.

Globant formed pods around functional areas of expertise, such as product info, user profiles, shopping cart, and checkout. Each pod had its own delivery goals (measured in story points) and each mid-level manager was responsible for the performance of two or three teams, receiving "awards" every time one of their teams achieved top performer status (compared to other teams). The main problem was that all the teams were measured with the same bar, but the pods were not all of the same size, and not all of them had what they needed to work effectively.

As the project began rolling, the client mandated bi-weekly meetings where the senior managers would recognize and congratulate the teams performing well. Unfortunately, the manager also identified and called out the teams not performing well according to the metrics and objectives. That generated a great deal of unease and led to systemic problems that negatively impacted the project.

"Managers started to make decisions just based on being able to reach and attain their designated goals," said Globant's project leader Maximiliano Trozzo. The problem was that focus played against other teams and the achievement of the overall project goals. "It created fighting between teams because of the pressure. It was a classic situation of 'me against the rest of the world,'" said Trozzo.

This management situation, intentional or not, made teams compete against each other, which in many occasions turned into "my team's needs are on top of everyone else's needs," said Trozzo.

Most of the time, the pods worked independently from

each other, but all the teams were still working on the same application, so at the end of the day, their work needed to integrate fully with the work of the other teams, which didn't always happen. On several occasions, one team broke the application in a way that halted the work of other teams. Other times, a team failed to deliver something that was needed by another team, making the second team also fail on their deliverables.

The situation imposed a challenge: how to have the teams work in an efficient and productive way without stepping over each other's boundaries. After many failed attempts, Globant came up with a mid-ground solution that satisfied all the persons involved. Through a continuous integration system and very strict quality metrics, whenever a team "broke" the build (in terms of continuous integration), all other teams were prevented from adding code to the repository (almost halting their work).

It may sound counterproductive that one team could be responsible for stopping the work of the other ten-plus teams, but it was actually better. Teams started to be more careful, making sure that their code worked before submitting it to the repository. This not only increased the quality of the code but also the teams' efficiency, as they were more likely to do things right from the beginning.

· The code repository got "healthier" because, at the most, only one build failure was present at any time.

- Having all the teams stop working at the same time increased the sensation of equality between teams, as everybody was effected equally.

- A team that would "break" something just to meet their deliverables was going to be much more exposed, so this practice stopped immediately.

The conclusion here is that through a strict process that sets boundaries and emphasizes accountability, a large number of teams managed to work together in an organized way and with better "overall" productivity than individual teams competing against each other. A new, healthier spirit of cooperation took hold, rather than a detrimental spirit of competition.

THE GAME OF DRILLING

IN THE WORLD of global oil exploration and drilling, there's a great deal of complexity when it comes to disparate types of data, which are difficult to coordinate and synthesize into meaningful information. Having talent that understands the specific industry and its nuances is essential when it comes to bringing a highly innovative software solution to market.

One oil drilling and services company, "O," wanted to improve the way it delivered services to its clients, creating a solution that would unify its distributed and multidisciplinary teams spread across several time zones and locations. The project was designed to solve a complex problem of coordinating communication and measuring the performance and quality of their service to clients. What's more, the company wanted the software to do all this in a simple and fluid way.

O's main business is fulfilling requests from oil companies to perform an analysis for drilling a well in a specific area. Partly because the company's services are worldwide, O had been experiencing communication problems based on differing languages, time zones, and data formatting and collection.

Globant assembled a pod comprised of engineers and designers that spanned many disciplines: gaming, interface design, web architecture, project management, visual design, and business analysis, including oil experts from Shanghai, China. The team headed into its work with the client with two IT engineers who helped sponsor the project and were excited to work with the team. And as often happens, there was a senior client manager who was skeptical about Globant's approach.

The pod members from Argentina and Shanghai scheduled certain business meetings in the US and met there for two weeks in order to discuss the status of the project. They focused on understanding the oil drilling company's business, its situation in the marketplace, and the goal for the project.

"After brainstorming, we proposed a Web dashboard

with different levels of abstraction," said Alejandro Lopez, Globant's project team director. They built the dashboard and assigned colors to indicate status, time line, and forum or chat communication. It provided a way to consolidate all the disparate documents and data formats into a single document.

But while most of the client members were thrilled with the solution, one member of the team wanted something more than the clickable prototype they'd designed and built. He wanted to push Globant and the pod to get even more creative when it came to the way the solution measured the quality of the service to the clients. With only three days left in the project, the VP client member extended the project an additional two days. The team worked furiously and came up with the idea of applying a gaming concept to the solution.

The pod decided to enhance the scoring of the project using color indicators to show if the project was taking longer than average. It assigned a scoring method so that each member of the project team could evaluate the solution. The team also decided to gamify the drilling project solution by setting a goal for a defined number of points before the team could send it to the client. What's more, this collaborative goal would also increase the interaction among team members in order to achieve a 100-point solution.

The solution impressed the client. The oil drilling services company said the gaming functions in the solution were particularly novel and above and beyond other types of products.

CRUISING SMART

I N 2013, Daniel Cespedes had eight years of professional engineering experience under his belt. His most recent job was as a software developer writing code for a telecommunications company's base stations. He started looking for a new opportunity where he could grow and face greater challenges. That's when Cespedes came across Globant, an innovative company that was growing fast and looked intriguing.

Cespedes was hired as a project manager to help a large entertainment and resort company, "R," create a new smartphone application for its cruise ships. Cespedes was in charge of all aspects of the project, including budget, scope, and communication with the customer.

"The big challenge was being able to deliver a new software product in a short span of a few months," Cespedes said.

Globant assembled a pod comprising its best technical people, with Cespedes as project manager. The pod had twelve people, two of whom were from R's staff and the rest, along with Cespedes, were Globant's developers, interface designers, and other functional experts. The pod started by building the first prototype to replace the cruise ship paper documents. Over the course of four sprints, each of which lasted two weeks, the pod was able to build the smartphone app for the client.

Part of what allowed this project to be accomplished so quickly was that Globant developed clear lines of communication within the pod and with client management. "We were able to establish a sense of trust with R," Cespedes said.

The pod metrics also helped convince R that Globant would continue to benefit the company. Of the assorted metrics, velocity was the most compelling one, demonstrating that the pod kept a strong pace. "Velocity gives you the idea of the productivity in a sprint," Cespedes said.

In the end, the smartphone application for vacationers aboard the vessels permitted them to chat with other people on the cruise, where cellular communication at sea was most often nonexistent because of the sheer distance to transmission towers on shore. The smartphone also helped passengers schedule activities on the ship, find information, make travel arrangements, map the ship and its course, and become oriented to its many offerings.

"There were many points of decision making where the outcome could have turned out entirely differently," Cespedes said. "The key was to assemble a pod with a correct skill mix and supported by the right maturity incentives to pull all the stops to create and deliver the right product."

At the end of the project, the client asked Globant to continue working on new features and additional products. Globant quickly set to work to scale the pods. The client wanted to create a center for excellence regarding mobile development. That translated into Globant needing to organize four teams.

As Globant's business with R expanded, so did Cespedes's

role in helping that business grow. He transitioned from a pod member to a core member, taking on more responsibilities and thus becoming the nucleus of new pods.

"I was told that, in Globant, you were the only one responsible for your career growth and, in Globant, you had all the opportunities you want," Cespedes said. "I was a little hesitant to believe this because I'd only experienced rigid, very structured companies without the opportunity to create a designated growth path."

But because of his success, he has continued to grow within the company. Cespedes now manages more than ten pods. "We are scaling the model and it's working very nicely."

RENDER ME SMOOTH

IN 2012, Globant began working with a large engineering software company, "E," to help improve its graphic engine. The software firm had not been able to find the talent it needed to do the project. It approached Globant to inquire about experts in rendering techniques.

The challenge for the client was to improve the rendering performance in its 2D/3D graphics engine. The underlying mathematics in the geometry engine were complex, with more than two million lines of code performing all kinds of calculations that included algorithms and data manipulations. For example, the engine could estimate the amount of light cast on the shape of a design after a certain type of change had been made. But the rendering engine was producing shapes with jagged lines instead of smooth lines, which was one of the problems to solve in the underlying engine. The project dynamics for the pod were further complicated by the members being spread across different time zones and cultures.

A pod was assembled comprising multidisciplinary skills with members that included a strong rendering team in Argentina, which interacted with the client's team members in San Francisco and Shanghai, China. The project got off on very strong footing with a good relationship with the teams, said Alejandro Lopez, Globant project director.

When the team got underway, there was no methodology for the complex 2D/3D engine. The software company had never used the agile methodology, but rather was wed to the waterfall process whereby the specifications are first generated before producing any design. The team started by implementing what is called a "scrum," an incremental test of the design.

After a few unsuccessful sprints, the pod found that it was never able to complete a sprint, which was complicated by the fact that the client changed the timing of the sprints. There were sprints of 140 story points. For a team like this, the typical amount of story points should be much lower. The decision was made to split the teams and have separated sprints of forty story points per sprint, which is more typical for two-week sprints. That created problems for maintaining consistency in the sprints and keeping a set of reliable metrics to estimate the scope of the project goals and time frame. What's more, the first agile approach failed despite having a strong communications plan in place. "We didn't achieve what we were planning," Lopez said. The pod was not even able to complete a single user story.

At that point, the team huddled and decided to shift from Scrum to Kanban in order to emphasize just-in-time delivery and to prevent the pod members from becoming overloaded and demotivated. A reality check is sometimes required to focus on the pod's improvement by stabilizing the process and reprocessing the maturity criteria. It took some convincing for the senior member of the client team, but eventually it was well received. It helped both the client and Globant grasp a better sense of the effort for the different task and work. New types of metrics helped distribute the work across teams, affording them greater independence while maintaining a strong team effort. The project paid big dividends to the client software company because it also gained insights about how it could better plan and manage future software development projects.

The pod started with a cycle time of eight days, and after identifying the bottlenecks and dependencies, the pod finished with a lead time of 4.5 days after a month of work. What's more, the pods were able to identify the Work in Progress (WIP) limit for each stage on the Kanban board. This was something that helped the team reduce the cycle time and also identify items that were far from the intended cycle time, which had a deviation of about two or even four weeks.

The overall benefit to the engineering software company was it could establish specific and reliable dates for the release of its software; in the past, those estimates were not as reliable. The project work helped the company gain greater efficiencies by reducing the number of bottlenecks and wait times.

MEETING THE BOTTOM LINE

A STEALTH STARTUP COMPANY, "X," had a common mix of problems that many companies face: limited funds and a short time-to-market window for getting their product launched. They couldn't afford to waste any time when it came to building a financial application and Web platform for consumers. In simple terms, they needed to hit the ground running and take advantage of a seasonal market opportunity.

X's two founders knew they had a strong concept. But they also recognized they needed help to build the platform and application module. The CEO had more than twenty years of software industry experience, and the co-founder had industry experience but no software product experience. The co-founder was in charge of the product development effort.

The immediate challenge was to put together a team to build the application. The CEO thought they already had the team they needed to build the back-end platform. They'd spent some of their startup capital to acquire a small engineering group to build the platform. He also wanted to make sure the platform had a tight minimum viable product (MVP) at launch and felt he had a clear picture of what the platform needed to deliver.

In contrast, the co-founder believed the platform served a slightly different purpose and different perspective from what the MVP needed to deliver. What's more, he was an advocate of the waterfall software process based on test-driven development (an approach in which you first write validation tests and then start coding against those tests). He was unfamiliar with and unsure of the "agile pod" methodology. That became a source of problems, as the desire to pursue a waterfall process and generate documentation before developing led to a speed bump at the beginning of the project, which is when the team should be accelerating, according to Peter Traugot, the Globant project leader.

"Whether or not a client has a grand idea about their desired goals, they only get to select two of the following areas for focus when it comes to building the product," said Traugot. "Those three elements are time, money, and scope."

The founders wanted to ensure that the platform was able to attract "real eyes" on their application experience as soon as possible. That would help afford time for the application and experience to go through several iterations and then be tested before it went to market.

Where problems started to arise was with X's team that was responsible for back-end software that would communicate with the platform and application. The trouble was that the back-end engineering team never supplied a plan nor identified the level of effort it needed. That meant the other team building the Web platform and application would have developed in a vacuum without ever knowing whether they'd met the back-end requirements, or whether they would be able to deliver on time or even at all, Traugot recalled. Without clarity and continuity of a product goal, X would have floundered for weeks if not months deciding who was on the right path.

Globant brought in a pod composed of a fully integrated team representing all required aspects of product development to address and solve all of these issues while maintaining full transparency and communication with the client. The communication was key to ensure X had complete exposure and control of the direction of the product. The pod would maintain velocity and "agile" responsiveness to feedback. The solution helped X move forward with its platform and application plans.

In retrospect, Traugot said, "Without having a target demographic looking at the product and experiencing the journey, X would never have had the feedback it needed to validate its approach." The company would have gone to market without having properly set the user experience.

PUBLISH OR PERISH

In 2013, a large consulting client, "C," wanted to engage Globant to help build an application that would complement its soon-to-be-released business book. The deadline for the release of the book was set, and the application would need to be built to meet that fixed deadline. The only problem was that C didn't know what kind of application it wanted to build to work synergistically with the material in the book.

A pod was assembled to take on the challenge. It was made up of junior members, which included a product manager, quality control person, and two groups of developers. The pod members were distributed in the United States and in four different regions of Argentina.

Expectations for the Globant team were high because of the consulting client's visibility and a very tough time-to-market requirement attached to the project. C did know that the book and the application were focused on the guiding principles about how exceptional companies perform and succeed.

The consulting firm had collected historical data on more than 25,000 companies and used that to help determine what made a company great. C had sixty years of data collected, from 1966 to 2010, that it used to help uncover the essential elements of high corporate achievement. It compiled a list of more than 300 companies and explored the key factors that made these companies exceptional in their industry.

C examined the companies and looked beyond regulation and competition. The main goal of the application was for readers who bought the book as a resource to prove the book's rules held up with all sorts of companies, not just those listed in the book. Users could see whether the metrics of their own businesses aligned with those of successful corporations.

"Those three rules correspond to a huge set of data and mathematical rules," said Mario Moreno, Globant project director. "The application only had to show different values and charts based on this set of data."

The pod got started and built the first prototype, which took one or two sprints, each two weeks long. At the beginning of the project, Globant didn't know how to calculate the specific values related to the historical data from this large set of companies.

"It wasn't until the middle of the project that the pod figured that problem out," Moreno said.

There were moments of pressure and uncertainty when the team had to make decisions to align their course. It helped that the communication between pod members was strong and fluid despite the distributed nature of the project.

The pod spent weekends and long days working on the project. More than two months later, the pod delivered its application to the client. It was well received. The client liked the prototype the pod showed them, especially how the application showcased the core principles from the book.

The project was not without typical mishaps, such as reshuffling of a pod member performing QA functions in the middle of the project, and one of the developers was let go. But the project ended well and on budget.

"Throughout the project, there were difficult calls with the consulting client in terms of meeting deadlines," Moreno said. "But the communication set up by the pod helped keep the team on track."

SOURCES

SOURCES

PREFACE:

Eku Baaskaeku, "About EA Corporation," Electronic Art blog, December 16, 2012, http://eabaaska.blogspot com/2012/12/about-ea-corporation.html.

CHAPTER 1: AGILE ECONOMICS

Paul R. La Monica, "Netflix is king of content…but it's still risky," CNN Money, February 3, 2015, http://money cnn.com/2015/02/03/investing/netflix-stock-surge-risks/.

Brent Lang, "Box Office: 'Guardians of the Galaxy' Astounds with $160.4 Mil Global Debut," *Variety*, August 3, 2014, http://variety.com/2014/film/news/box-office guardians-of-the-galaxy-astounds-with-160-4-mil global-debut-1201274534/.

Pamela McClintock, "Box Office: Universal's '47 Ronin' Likely to Result in $175 Million Loss," *The Hollywood Reporter*, December 27, 2013, http://www. hollywoodreporter.com/news/box-office-universals-47-ronin-667771.

Donald Sull and Kathleen M. Eisenhardt, "Netflix's 'House of Cards' secrets: The real story behind Kevin Spacey and Frank Underwood's meteoric ascent," Salon.com, April 26, 2015, http://www.salon.com/2015/04/26/netflixs_house_of_cards_secrets_the_real_story_behind_kevin_spacey_and_frank_underwoods_meteoric_ascent/.

CHAPTER 2: WHAT'S WRONG WITH SOFTWARE

Tim Brown, *Change by Design: How Design Thinking Transforms Organizations and Inspires Innovation* (New York: HarperBusiness, 2009).

Thomas Lockwood, *Design Thinking: Integrating Innovation, Customer Experience, and Brand Value* (New York: Allworth Press, 2009).

Lars Mieritz, "Survey Shows Why Projects Fail," Gartner.com, June 1, 2012, https://www.gartner.com/doc/2034616 survey-shows-projects-fail.

"Why Tech Projects Fail: 5 Unspoken Reasons," InformationWeek.com, April 4, 2013, http:www.informationweek.com/it-leadership/why-tech-projects-fail-5-unspoken-reasons/d/d-id/1109399?page_number=1.

CHAPTER 3: WHAT IS DIGITAL SUCCESS

Driek Desmet, Ewan Duncan, Jay Scanlan, and Marc Singer, "The Six Building Blocks for Creating a High-Performing Digital Enterprise," McKinsey

& Company, September 2015, http://www.
mckinsey.com/insights/organization/six_building_
blocks_for_creating_a_high_performing_digital_
enterprise.

Watts S. Humphrey, "Characterizing the software process:
A maturity framework," PDF presented by
Software Engineering Institute, Carnegie Mellon
University, March 1988, http://www.sei.cmu.edu/
reports/87tr011.pdf.

Rajeev Syal, "Abandoned NHS IT system has cost £10bn so
far," *The Guardian*, September 13, 2013, http://www.
theguardian.com/society/2013/sep/18/nhs-records-
system-10bn.

CHAPTER 4: HOW PODS DELIVER DIGITAL TRANSFORMATION

Ron Adner, *The Wide Lens: A New Strategy for Innovation*
(New York: Portfolio, 2013).

Walter Isaacson, *The Innovators: How a Group of Hackers,
Geniuses, and Geeks Created the Digital Revolution*
(New York: Simon & Schuster, 2015).

CHAPTER 5: SEEDING AND SCALING PODS

Ralph Waldo Emerson, from "Essays: First Series (1841),"
http://www.emersoncentral.com/history.htm.

Lewis Thomas, *Lives of a Cell: Notes of a Biology Watcher*
(New York: Penguin Books, 1978).

CHAPTER 6 THE POWER OF METRICS

Randall Beck and James Hartner, "Why Good Managers Are So Rare," *Harvard Business Review*, March 13, 2014, https://hbr.org/2014/03/why-good-managers-are-so-rare/.

Bernard Ferrari and Jessica Goethals, "Using Rivalry to Spur Innovation," McKinsey & Company, May 2010.

"Pioneering: Sustaining U.S. Leadership in Space," Space Foundation, December 2012, http://www.spacefoundation.org/programs/research-and-analysis/pioneering.

"Q-12 Meta-Analysis," Gallup research survey, September 22, 2014, http://www.gallup.com/services/177047/q12-meta-analysis.aspx.

Philippe Siberzahn and Walter Van Dyck, *The Balancing Act of Innovation* (Belgium: Lannoo Publishers, 2011).

CHAPTER 7: IT'S IN THE GAME

Randall Beck and James Hartner, "Why Good Managers Are So Rare," *Harvard Business Review*, March 13, 2014, https://hbr.org/2014/03/why-good-managers-are-so-rare/.

Gareth Cook, "Sebastian Seung's Quest to Map the Human Brain," *The New York Times* magazine, Jan 8, 2015, http://www.nytimes.com/2015/01/11/magazine/sebastian-seungs-quest-to-map-the-human-brain.html?_r=0.

"How to Foster Innovation," National Innovation Initiative (NII) 2012 study, published by the Council on Competitiveness, Washington, D.C.

Jane McGonigal, *Reality is Broken: Why Games Make Us Better and How They Can Change the World* (New York: Penguin, 2011)

CHAPTER 8: ACHIEVING SOMETHING BIGGER

"Creating a Culture of Innovation," Google International Document, https://www.google.com/work/apps/business/learn-more/creating_a_culture_of_innovation.html.

Daniel Pink, *Drive: The Surprising Truth About What Motivates Us* (New York: Riverhead Books 2011).

Robyn Reilly, "Five Ways to Improve Employee Engagement Now," January 2014, http://www.gallup.com/businessjournal/166667/five-ways-improve-employee-engagement.aspx.

CHAPTER 9: WHAT'S NEXT

Tim Brown, *Change by Design: How Design Thinking Transforms Organizations and Inspires Innovation* (HarperCollins e-books, 2009).

Tanguy Catlin, Jay Scanlan, and Paul Willmott, "Raising your digital quotient," *McKinsey Quarterly*, June 2015, http://www.mckinsey.com/insights/strategy/raising_your_digital_quotient.

Walter Isaacson, *The Innovators: How a Group of Hackers, Geniuses, and Geeks Created the Digital Revolution* (New York: Simon & Schuster, 2015).

Cliff Kuang, "Disney's $1 Billion Bet on a Magical
      Wristband," *Wired*, http://www.wired.com/2015/03/
      disney-magicband/.

Mark A. Lemley, "The Myth of the Sole Inventor," Stanford
      Public Law Working Paper No. 1856610, July
      21, 2001, http://papers.ssrn.com/sol3/papers.
      cfm?abstract_id=1856610.

James Manyika, Jacques Bughin, Susan Lund, Olivia
      Nottebohm, David Poulter, Sebastian Jauch, and
      Sree Ramaswamy, "Global flows in a digital age,"
      McKinsey Global Institute, April 2014, http://www.
      mckinsey.com/insights/globalization/global_flows_
      in_a_digital_age.

James Manyika, Michael Chui, Jacques Bughin, Richard Dobbs,
      Peter Bisson, and Alex Marrs, "Disruptive technologies:
      Advances that will transform life, business, and the
      global economy," McKinsey Global Institute, March
      2013, http://www.mckinsey.com/insights/business_
      technology/disruptive_technologies.

EPILOGUE: THE NEW DIGITAL DESIGN GUILD

"How to Foster Innovation," National Innovation Initiative
      (NII) 2012 study, published by the Council on
      Competitiveness, Washington, D.C.

Thomas Lockwood, *Design Thinking: Integrating Innovation,
      Customer Experience, and Brand Value* (New York:
      Allworth Press, 2009).

GLOSSARY
TERMS AND DEFINITIONS

GLOSSARY

Terms and Definitions

AGILE SOFTWARE DEVELOPMENT: A set of fundamental principles about how software should be developed based on an agile way of working in contrast to previous heavy-handed software development methodologies.

BACKLOG: A collection of stories and tasks the sprint team will work on at some point in the future. Either the product owner has not prioritized them or has assigned them lower priority. Teams or organizations may use the term "backlog" in one of the following four ways:

1. Stories or tasks that are likely to be considered in the next iteration's planning game.

2. Stories or tasks that are definitely planned to be worked on in the next iteration (rather than just being available for consideration).

3. Stories or tasks that are assigned to the current iteration, but are not yet being worked on. As the team has time, these will be worked on after the higher-priority items are completed.

4. In a very fluid team, the planning game may assign more stories than can be done during the iteration. The backlog consists of stories and tasks that may slip into the next iteration.

BUILD PROCESS: The amount of variability in implementation makes it difficult to come up with a tight definition of a build process, but we would say that a build process takes source code and other configuration data as input and produces artifacts (sometimes called derived objects) as output. The exact number and definition of steps depends greatly on the types of inputs (Java versus C/C++ versus Perl/Python/ Ruby source code) and the type of desire output (CD image, downloadable zip file, or self-extracting binary, etc.). When the source code includes a compiled language, then the build process would certainly include a compilation and perhaps a linking step.

BUSINESS PROCESS MODELING (BPM): The activity of representing processes of an enterprise, so that the current ("as is") process may be analyzed and improved in future ("to be").

CAPABILITY MATURITY MODEL (CMM): In software engineering, CMM is a model of the maturity of the capability of certain business processes. A maturity model can be described as a structured collection of elements that describe certain aspects of maturity in an organization and aids in the definition and understanding of an organization's processes.

CHANGE MANAGEMENT: A field of management focused on organizational changes that aims to ensure that methods and procedures are used for efficient and prompt handling of all changes to controlled IT infrastructure in order to minimize the number and impact of any related incidents upon service.

COST ENGINEERING: The area of engineering practice where engineering judgment and experience are used in the application of scientific principles and techniques to problems of cost estimating, cost control, business planning and management science, profitability analysis, project management, and planning and scheduling.

DIGITAL JOURNEY: A context-aware interaction between an end user and a brand or business whereby the interaction becomes a digital conversation in which technology establishes and builds a powerful experience with deep emotional connections through three key values: simplification, surprise, and anticipation.

DIGITAL NATIVE: A person or a company born in the digital era and defined by their approach to technology that embraces a lean software practice willing to try, fail, and try again with an entrepreneurial startup. Also can be an innovative technology company whose new products re-redefine, drastically boost user experience and engagement. The term is attributed to educational consultant Marc Prensky, who coined it to refer to children raised in a digital, media-saturated world who require a media-rich learning environment to hold their attention

DEVOPS: The clipped compound of "development" and "operations" is a software development method that stresses communication, collaboration, integration, automation, and measurement of cooperation between software developers and other information-technology (IT) professionals.

GAMIFICATION: The approach and process of creating a game environment and then utilizing gaming technologies to boost and improve the overall productivity of developer teams. By doing so, team members can collaborate and bridge divisions between creative and engineering teams and establish a richer, more flexible integration of varied technology skill sets.

GOPODS: Globant's pod tool, which integrates with several other development tools and pulls specific standard metrics to help track and monitor various parameters, such as productivity, quality, and velocity in a software development project.

ITERATION: A period (from one week to two months in duration) during which the agile development team produces an increment of completed software. All system life cycle phases (requirements, design, code, and test) must be completed during the iteration and then (empirically) demonstrated for the iteration to be accepted as successfully completed. At the beginning of the iteration, the business or the product owner identifies the next (highest priority) chunk of work for the team to complete. The development team then estimates the level of effort and commits to completing a segment of work during the iteration. During the iteration, the team is not expected to change objectives or respond to change requests. However, at the front end of the next iteration the business or product owner is free to identify any new segment of work as the current highest priority.

ITERATIVE AND INCREMENTAL DEVELOPMENT: A cyclic software development process developed in response to the weaknesses of the waterfall model. It starts with an initial planning and ends with deployment with the cyclic interaction in between.

KANBAN: A tool derived from lean manufacturing associated with the branch of agile practices loosely referred to as Lean software development. Like a task board, Kanban visually represents the state of work in process. Unlike a task board, the Kanban constrains how much work in process is permitted to occur at the same time. The purpose of limiting work in process is to reduce bottlenecks and increase throughput by optimizing that segment of the value stream that is the subject of the Kanban. A principle difference between Kanban and Scrum is that Scrum limits work in process through timeboxing (i.e. the sprint) and Kanban limits work in process by limiting how much work may occur at one time (e.g. N tasks or N stories).

POD TEMPLATE COMPLIANCE: A pod template defines the composition of a pod in terms of roles and specific experience.

Each pod type (solution, development, evolution, devops) has an associated template. This is done to make sure guidelines are followed and that there's a balanced set of roles. For example, a solutions pod needs to have product and design roles, as described in the template. If a solutions pod is weak in design, then it will not be compliant with the solution pod template.

PROJECT ACCOUNTING is the practice of creating financial reports specifically designed to track the financial progress of projects, which can then be used by managers to aid project management.

PROJECT COST MANAGEMENT: A method of managing a project in real time from the estimating stage to project control through the use of technology, cost, schedule, and monitoring productivity.

PROJECT MANAGEMENT SOFTWARE: A type of software, including scheduling, cost control and budget management, resource allocation, collaboration software, communication, quality management, and documentation or administration systems, which are used to deal with the complexity of large projects.

SCRUM: A daily team meeting held to provide a status update to the team members. The "semi-real-time" status allows participants to know about potential challenges as well as coordinate efforts to resolve difficult and/or time-consuming issues. The meetings are usually timeboxed to five to fifteen minutes and are held standing up to remind people to keep the meeting short and to the point.

SENIORITY RATIO: The percentage of experienced pod members who are considered "senior." Seniority is generally defined by the number of years of experience in technology or management positions. This differs from "Core member ratio," as core members are those who have specific experience in being part of a pod and working within the context of one or more digital journeys for a client.

SPRINT: The scrum term for an iteration. The sprint starts with a sprint planning meeting. At the end of the sprint there is a sprint review meeting, followed by a sprint retrospective meeting.

STORY: A requirement, feature, and/or unit of business value that can be estimated and tested. Stories describe work that must be done to create and deliver a feature for a product. Stories are the basic unit of communication, planning, and negotiation between the scrum team, business owners, and the product owner. Stories consist of the following elements:

1. A description, usually in business terms.

2. A size, for rough estimation purposes, generally expressed in story points (such as 1, 2, 3, 5).

3. An acceptance test, giving a short description of how the story will be validated.

STORY POINT: The story-point unit of measurement describes a user scenario that involves some kind of interaction between some form of software and a user, or another system. Sizing product features in story points helps a pod estimate product size, complexity, and its derivatives, such as velocity and cost.

VELOCITY: Measures how much work a team can complete in an iteration. Velocity is often measured in stories or story points, or it could also measure tasks in hours or an equivalent unit. Velocity is used to measure how long it will take a particular team to deliver future outcomes by extrapolating on the basis of its prior performance. This works in agile development, when work is comprehensively completed after each iteration.

Glossary terms were culled from : http://www.solutionsiq.com/agile-glossary/ and http://en.wikipedia.org/wiki/Glossary_of_project_management

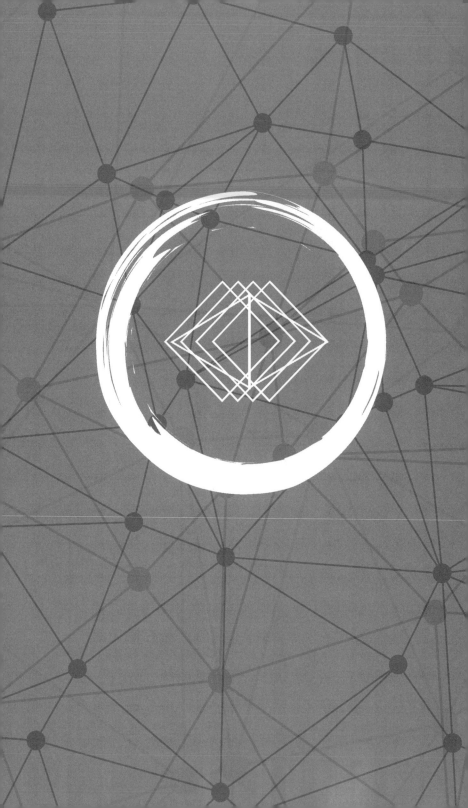

AFTERWORD
GoPods & StarMeUp

AFTERWORD
GoPods & StarMeUp

GoPods and StarMeUp are two of the tools that enable us to monitor things as we evolve with our digital journeys and the podification of our teams. GoPods is a tool that sits on top of regular project-tracking tools and combines this information from that of other sources, such as build-management tools, code-quality platforms, etc, and provides a view for all of the pods working together to track their progress, productivity, quality, and autonomy.

Along with the tracking of these individual metrics, GoPods enables managers to define and track the maturity of their teams. As the pod matures, a sense of recognition and belonging is established.

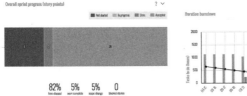

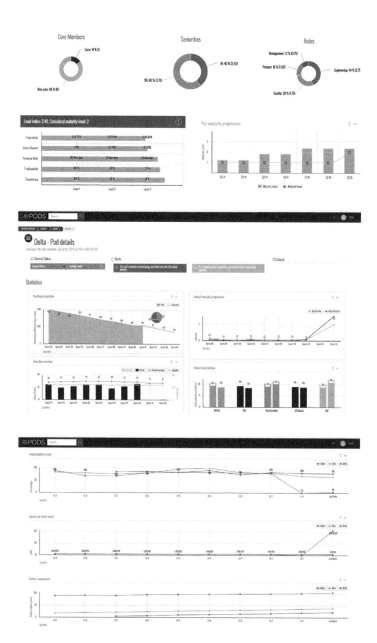

S TARMEUP integrates different features in a gamified platform. Allowing peer-to-peer recognition and reviews along with continuous monitoring, all in a scalable, social, and interactive way. Enhance social interaction between peers, identify reliable employees, and get up-to-date metrics in a fast and easy way.

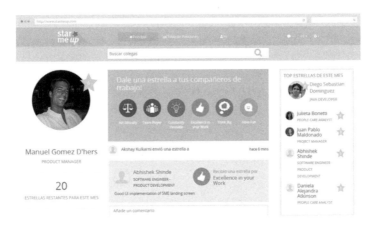

The activity builds communities and enhances social interaction between peers. Employees feel they are part of something bigger. Engagement between employees increases business performance in all areas of the business.

StarMeUp promotes people's happiness at work. It motivates them to be engaged in the company's vision with each star representing a key aspect of the corporate values. Employees feel an overall sense of recognition and belonging.

Using game mechanics, the leaderboard, with up-to-date metrics, can create healthy competition. Top performers get rewards and recognition company-wide. While employees enjoy a sense of belonging to something bigger, the leaderboard helps identify leaders in the company based on peer-to-peer and manager reviews.

ACKNOWLEDGMENTS
From the Authors

THE *NEVER-ENDING JOURNEY* has been a team effort, agile to the extreme! It is exciting to see how several weeks of hard work came true in *The Never-Ending Digital Journey* and resulted in a book that represents the essence of Globant's vision and of how we see the future of businesses. It was an extremely rewarding process; we hope that every reader enjoys the outcome as much as we have enjoyed writing it.

Our thanks to Lee Bruno, our partner in writing this book, who worked with us side by side, polishing and making sense of every word, putting up with multiple points of views, changes of mind, and many revisions.

Special thanks to all the Globers who participated with ideas and actual implementations of digital journeys with agile pods. They refined the model by doing, to a form that we can now showcase. Also, we would like to express our appreciation for the time and effort of those Globers who wrote success cases to illustrate pods in a practical setting.

MARTÍN MIGOYA

My most valuable thanks to my family. My wonderful wife Carolina and my sons Facundo, Manuel and Felipe are my strongest pillars and have been my main source of inspiration during Globant's exciting journey. These past 12 years have been filled with joy; and our story could have not been possible without my family's endless and unlimited faith and support.

GUIBERT ENGLEBIENNE

I'd like to thank my wife, Alita, and my daughters Sofia and Claire, for being there for me at all times. They always believed in me and joined me while I pursued some of my craziest dreams. It is because of them that I have been able to be a part of Globant's founding team with all the late nights and efforts it meant.

ANDRÉS ANGELANI

I deeply thank my family; my beloved wife, Laura, and the light of our lives: Emma, Dante, Valentino, and Siena. They supported this effort despite the many number of weekend and nighttime hours I spent on my laptop and away from home. It has been an exciting ride only possible thanks to their love and support.

THE NEVER ENDING DIGITAL JOURNEY

Managing editor: Lee Bruno
Editor: Jan Hughes
Copy editor: Michelle Dotter
Book and jacket design: Iain R. Morris
Design assistant: Suzi Hutsell

ISBN: 978-1-937359-92-8

Printed in the United States of America
10 9 8 7 6 5 4 3 2 1

Roundtree Press
6 Petaluma Blvd. North, Suite B-6
Petaluma, CA 94952

(707) 769 1617
www.roundtreepress.com